HUTCHINSON POCKET

Dictionary of
Computing
and
Multimedia

Other titles in the Hutchinson Pocket series:

HUTCHINSON POCKET

Dictionary of
Computing
and
Multimedia

Helicon

Copyright © Helicon Publishing Ltd 1995

Helicon Publishing Ltd
42 Hythe Bridge Street
Oxford OX1 2EP

Printed and bound in Great Britain by
Unwin Brothers Ltd, Old Woking, Surrey

ISBN 1–85986–106–7

British Cataloguing in Publication Data

A catalogue record for this book is available
from the British Library

Editorial director
Michael Upshall

Managing editor
Sara Jenkins-Jones

Project editor
Catherine Thompson

Contributors
Wendy Grossman
Ian Kingston
David Penfold
Jack Schofield

Art and design
Terence Caven

Production
Tony Ballsdon

Introduction

Computing and multimedia in the 1990s

Buying a computer has never been simpler. Almost every customer, large or small, wants an IBM PC-compatible with an Intel 486 processor, four megabytes of RAM, Super VGA colour screen and Microsoft Windows 3.1 software. There are variations – faster processors, bigger hard discs and screens, more memory – but the market has a working standard: one that has made Microsoft and Intel very rich; one that is being extended, and challenged.

Beyond the desktop

Microsoft, Intel and numerous PC manufacturers want to expand beyond the desktop. Firms like Grid and NCR are selling battery-powered, portable 'pen-driven' computers for people who don't need a keyboard – van drivers making deliveries, or field service engineers. They can use PCs with power-saving processors and Microsoft's Windows for Pen Computing. Home users can have interactive CD players with infrared controllers and Microsoft's Modular Windows. Corporate users can have multiprocessor 'servers' using Windows NT (New Technology) to replace minicomputers and small mainframes. RAID (redundant arrays of inexpensive discs) storage systems use multiple PC hard drives instead of large, expensive, mainframe discs.

Modular systems comprising PC processors and drives appeal to a market where large computers have been expensive and incompatible. Since PCs sell in large volumes, intense competition and economies of scale have driven down prices, and propagated a huge range of software. But some suppliers offer faster processors than Intel, and operating systems designed for specific tasks, without the inevitable compromises of standardization.

Many firms have produced reduced instruction set computer (RISC) processors – simpler and faster than traditional designs like Intel's x86 line. Examples include AT&T's Hobbit, DEC's Alpha, the ARM (Acorn Risc Machine), Hewlett-Packard's Precision Architecture, Mips' R4000, and Sun's Sparc (scalable processor architecture). The Sparc chip is the most popular, but the market is confusing and confused. There is a plethora of alternative operating systems exploiting these various chips. One is Go's PenPoint, which AT&T, IBM and others are adopting for pen-driven computers and personal communicators. On minis and workstations, Unix is becoming dominant but, instead of backing the industry-standard Unix System V Release 4, several firms have developed variants, confusing the market and introducing unnecessary incompatibilities. The resulting 'Unix wars' over the last five years have provided Microsoft's NT with its opportunity. Paradoxically, the challenges to Intel and Microsoft have reinforced the PC's appeal. The slogan is: 'evolution not revolution'. When fast PCs are so cheap, why take a risk?

CD-ROM

The biggest development is CD-ROM (compact disc, read-only memory). One disc can store more than 600 megabytes of data, equivalent to 450 standard floppies or 150 million words of text. Prices are low, because the industry benefits from the R&D investment and high-volume production facilities for audio CD, with which CD-ROM is compatible.

A large operating system or suite of programs, occupying from 25 to 80 or more floppy discs, can be packed onto a single CD. 'Multimedia' programs can be produced, with digital data, sound, still and moving images on the same disc. Typical discs include dictionaries which have pictures and can say the words you look up, atlases including national anthems, and encyclopedias with moving diagrams. Computer games are also appearing on CD-ROM.

Suppliers have started 'format wars' that make the VHS–Betamax video battle look trivial. Most CD-ROMs are designed for a specific system; there are products for PCs and Apple Macintoshes, Sun workstations, Commodore Amigas (the CDTV system), Fujitsu's FM-Towns, and Sega Megadrive and NEC games consoles. There are other consumer offerings, including CD-I (compact disc-interactive) from Philips and Sony, PhotoCD from Philips and Kodak, the Video Information System from Tandy and Zenith, and Sony's Electronic Book. There is also a recordable format, CD-R.

Millions of CD-ROM drives will be sold for Sega, Nintendo and NEC games consoles, but the emerging standards are CD-I (incorporating PhotoCD) and MPC, the Microsoft-backed Multimedia Personal Computer specification based on Windows 3. CD-I systems look like high-end CD players: they plug into a TV set, and can be used for audio CDs as well as multimedia programs. MPC systems are usually 386SX-based PCs upgraded with CD-ROM drive, sound card and, usually, two small stereo loudspeakers. The CD-ROM drive should be able to play 'multi-session' discs (enabling it to handle Photo CD discs, holding more than one set of pictures) and have XA (extended architecture) capabilities, to interleave sound with graphics.

The original PC was expensive, and its handling of colour graphics and sound primitive, limiting its appeal to the business market. The MPC is becoming affordable and suitable for use in homes and schools, ushering in a new age of electronic books in which people can speak, cows can moo, cartoons can be animated, and you can display the text any size you like. CDs of plays, operas and musicals can have moving video clips plus the libretto and score. Viewers will become interactive participants, making 'director's cuts' of films, steering plot-lines or choosing their own endings. Offered such power, will anyone want to resist?

A

absolute (of a value) in computing, real and unchanging. For example, an *absolute address* is a location in memory and an *absolute cell reference* is a single fixed cell in a spreadsheet display. The opposite of absolute is ◊relative.

accelerator board type of ◊expansion board that makes a computer run faster. It usually contains an additional ◊central processing unit.

access the way in which ◊file access is provided so that the data can be stored, retrieved, or updated by the computer.

access time or *reaction time* the time taken by a computer, after an instruction has been given, to read from or write to ◊memory.

accumulator a special register, or memory location, in the ◊arithmetic and logic unit of the computer processor. It is used to hold the result of a calculation temporarily or to store data that is being transferred.

Acorn UK computer manufacturer. In the early 1980s, Acorn produced a series of home microcomputers, including the Electron and the Atom. Its most successful computer, BBC Microcomputer, was produced in conjunction with the BBC. Subsequent computers (the Master and the ◊Archimedes) were less successful. Acorn was taken over by the Italian company Olivetti 1985.

acoustic coupler device that enables computer data to be transmitted and received through a normal telephone handset; the handset rests on the coupler to make the connection. A small speaker within the device is used to convert the computer's digital output data into sound signals, which are then picked up by the handset and transmitted through the telephone system. At the receiving telephone, a second acoustic coupler or modem converts the sound signals back into digital data for input into a computer.

Unlike a ◊modem, an acoustic coupler does not require direct connection to the telephone system. However, interference from background noise means that the quality of transmission is poorer than with a modem, and more errors are likely to arise.

Acrobat coding system developed by Adobe Systems for ◊electronic publishing applications. Acrobat coding can be generated directly from ◊PostScript files.

Ada high-level computer-programming language, developed and owned by the US Department of Defense, designed for use in situations in which a computer directly controls a process or machine, such as a military aircraft. The language took more than five years to specify, and became commercially available only in the late 1980s. It is named after English mathematician Ada Augusta Byron (1815–1851).

ADC in electronics, abbreviation for *◊analogue-to-digital converter*.

adder electronic circuit in a computer or calculator that carries out the process of adding two binary numbers. A separate adder is needed for each pair of binary ◊bits to be added. Such circuits are essential components of a computer's ◊arithmetic and logic unit (ALU).

address in a computer memory, a number indicating a specific location. At each address, a single piece of data can be stored. For microcomputers, this normally amounts to one ◊byte (enough to represent a single character, such as a letter or digit).

The maximum capacity of a computer memory depends on how many memory addresses it can have. This is normally measured in units of 1,024 bytes (known as kilobytes, or K).

address bus the electrical pathway or ◊bus used to select the route for any particular data item as it is moved from one part of a computer to another.

AI abbreviation for *◊artificial intelligence*.

Aiken Howard (Hathaway) 1900–   . US mathematician and computer pioneer. In 1939, in conjunction with engineers from ◊IBM, he started work on the design of an automatic calculator using standard business-machine components. In 1944 the team completed one of the first computers, the Automatic Sequence Controlled Calculator (known as the Harvard Mark I), a programmable computer controlled by punched paper tape and using ◊punched cards.

Aiken was born in Hoboken, New Jersey, and studied engineering at the University of Wisconsin. His early research at Harvard in the 1930s was sponsored by the Navy Board of Ordnance and in 1939 he and three IBM engineers were placed under contract to develop a machine to produce mathematical tables and to assist the ballistics and gunnery divisions of the military.

The Harvard Mark I was principally a mechanical device, although it had a few electronic features; it was 15 m/49 ft long and 2.5 m/8 ft high, and weighed more than 30 tonnes. Addition took 0.3 sec, multiplication 4 sec. It was able to manipulate numbers of up to 23 decimal places and to store 72 of them. The Mark II, completed 1947, was a fully electronic machine, requiring only 0.2 sec for addition and 0.7 sec for multiplication. It could store 100 ten-digit figures and their signs.

ALGOL (acronym for *algo*rithmic *l*anguage) an early high-level programming language, developed in the 1950s and 1960s for scientific applications. A general-purpose language, ALGOL is best suited to mathematical work and has an algebraic style. Although no longer in common use, it has greatly influenced more recent languages, such as Ada and PASCAL.

algorithm procedure or series of steps that can be used to solve a problem.

In computer science, it describes the logical sequence of operations to be performed by a program. A ◊flow chart is a visual representation of an algorithm.

The word derives from the name of 9th-century Arab mathematician Muhammad ibn-Mūsā al- Khwārizmī.

aliasing effect seen on computer screen or printer output, when smooth curves appear to made up of steps because the resolution is not high enough. ◊Antialiasing is a software technique that reduces this effect by using intermediate shades of colour to create an apparently smoother curve.

alpha a 64-bit ◊RISC chip launched 1993 by Digital Equipment (DEC). It was seen as a rival to Intel's ◊Pentium chip.

alphanumeric data data made up of any of the letters of the alphabet and any digit from 0 to 9. The classification of data according to the type or types of character contained enables computer ◊validation systems to check the accuracy of data: a computer can be programmed to reject entries that contain the wrong type of character. For example, a person's name would be rejected if it contained any numeric data, and a bank-account number would be rejected if it contained any alphabetic data. A car's registration number, by comparison, would be expected to contain alphanumeric data but no punctuation marks.

ALU abbreviation for ◊*arithmetic and logic unit*.

American National Standards Institute (ANSI) US national standards body. It sets official procedures in (among other areas) computing and electronics. The ANSI ◊character set is the standard set of characters used by Windows-based computers.

Amiga microcomputer produced by US company Commodore 1985 to succeed the Commodore C64 home computer. The original Amiga was based on the Motorola 68000 microprocessor and achieved significant success in the domestic market.

Despite a failure to sell to the general business market, the latest versions of the Amiga are widely used in the film and video industries, where the Amiga's specialized graphics capabilities are used to create a variety of visual effects.

analogue (of a quantity or device) changing continuously; by contrast a ◊digital quantity or device varies in series of distinct steps. For example, an analogue clock measures time by means of a continuous movement of hands around a dial, whereas a digital clock measures time with a numerical display that changes in a series of discrete steps.

Most computers are digital devices. Therefore, any signals and data from a analogue device must be passed through a suitable ◊analogue-to-digital converter before they can be received and processed by computer. Similarly, output signals from digital computers must be passed through a digital-to-analogue converter before they can be received by an analogue device.

analogue computer computing device that performs calculations through the interaction of continuously varying physical quantities, such as voltages (as distinct from the more common ◊digital computer, which works with discrete quantities). An analogue computer is said to operate in real time (corresponding to time in the real world), and can therefore be used to monitor and control other events as they happen.

Although common in engineering since the 1920s, analogue computers are not general-purpose computers, but specialize in solving differential calculus and similar mathematical problems. The earliest analogue computing device is thought to be the flat, or planispheric, astrolabe, which originated in about the 8th century.

analogue-to-digital converter (ADC) electronic circuit that converts an analogue signal into a digital one. Such a circuit is needed to convert the signal from an analogue device into a digital signal for input into a computer. For example, many ◊sensors designed to measure physical quantities, such as temperature and pressure, produce an

analogue-to-digital converter

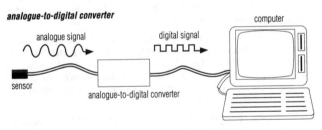

analogue signal in the form of voltage and this must be passed through an ADC before computer input and processing. A ◊digital-to-analogue converter performs the opposite process.

analyst job classification for ◊computer personnel. An analyst prepares a report on an existing data processing system and makes proposals for changes and improvements.

AND gate in electronics, a type of ◊logic gate.

ANSI abbreviation for ◊*American National Standards Institute*, a US national standards body.

antialiasing in computer graphics, a software technique for diminishing 'jaggies' – steplike lines that should be smooth. Jaggies occur because the output device, the monitor or printer, does not have a high enough resolution to represent a smooth line. Antialiasing reduces the prominence of jaggies by surrounding the steps with intermediate shades of grey (for grey-scaling devices) or colour (for colour devices). Although this reduces the jagged appearance of the lines, it also makes them fuzzier.

API abbreviation for ◊*Applications Program Interface*, a standard environment in which computer programs are written.

Apple US computer company, manufacturer of the ◊Macintosh range of computers.

application a program or job designed for the benefit of the end user, such as a payroll system or a ◊word processor. The term is used to distinguish such programs from those that control the computer (◊systems programs) or assist the programmer, such as a ◊compiler.

applications package in computing, the set of programs and related documentation (such as instruction manuals) used in a particular application. For example, a typical payroll applications package would consist of separate programs for the entry of data, updating the master files, and printing the pay slips, plus documentation in the form of program details and instructions for use.

Applications Program Interface (API) standard environment, including tools, protocols, and other routines, in which programs can be written. An API ensures that all applications are consistent with the operating system and have a similar ◊user interface.

Archie software tool for locating information on the ◊Internet. It can be difficult to locate a particular file because of the relatively unstructured nature of the Internet. Archie uses indexes of files and their locations on the Internet to find them quickly.

Archimedes microcomputer introduced by ◊Acorn 1987. It was based on a ◊RISC microprocessor called the ◊ARM, and was intended to be the successor to Acorn's BBC Microcomputer. Despite its technically advanced design, it did not prove successful.

argument the value on which a ◊function operates. For example, if the argument 16 is operated on by the function 'square root', the answer 4 is produced.

arithmetic and logic unit (ALU) in a computer, the part of the ◊central processing unit (CPU) that performs the basic arithmetic and logic operations on data.

ARM (abbreviation for *Advanced RISC Machine*) microprocessor developed by Acorn 1985 for use in the ◊Archimedes microcomputer. In 1990 the company Advanced RISC Machines was formed to develop the ARM microprocessor. The ARM is the microprocessor used in Apple's ◊Newton.

ARPAnet (acronym for *Advanced Research Projects Agency Network*) early US network that forms the basis of the ◊Internet. It was set up 1969 by ARPA to provide services to US academic institutions and commercial organizations conducting computer science research. ARPAnet pioneered many of today's networking techniques.

It was renamed DARPAnet when ARPA changed its name to Defense Advanced Research Projects Agency. In 1975 responsibility for DARPAnet was passed on to the Defense Communication Agency.

array in computer programming, a list of values that can all be referred to by a single ◊variable name. Separate values are distinguished by using a *subscript* with each variable name.

For example, consider this list of highest daily temperatures:

temperature (°C)	
day 1	22
day 2	23
day 3	19
day 4	21

This array might be stored with the single variable name 'temp'. Separate elements of the array would then be identified with subscripts.

So, for example, the array element 'temp$_{(1)}$' would store the value '22', and the array element 'temp$_{(3)}$' would store the value '19'.

An array may use more than one subscript. For example, consider this list showing the number of pints of milk delivered to four houses:

	house 1	house 2	house 3	house 4
day 1	2	2	3	1
day 2	2	1	2	1
day 3	3	2	0	1
day 4	2	1	2	1
day 5	4	1	2	2
day 6	4	5	4	4

If the array were given the variable name 'pint', its elements would be identified with two subscripts: one for the house and one for the day of the week. So, for example, the array element 'pints$_{(2, 6)}$' would store the value '5', and the array element 'pints$_{(3, 3)}$' would store the value '0'.

Arrays are useful because they allow programmers to write general routines that can process long lists of data. For example, if every price stored in an accounting program used a different variable name, separate program instructions would be needed to process each price. However, if all the prices were stored in an array, a general routine could be written to process, say, 'price(J)', and, by allowing J to take different values, could then process any individual price.

artificial intelligence (AI) branch of science concerned with creating computer programs that can perform actions comparable with those of an intelligent human. Current AI research covers such areas as planning (for robot behaviour), language understanding, pattern recognition, and knowledge representation.

Early AI programs, developed in the 1960s, attempted simulations of human intelligence or were aimed at general problem-solving techniques. It is now thought that intelligent behaviour depends as much on the knowledge a system possesses as on its reasoning power. Present emphasis is on ◊knowledge-based systems, such as ◊expert systems.

ASCII (acronym for *American standard code for information interchange*) a coding system in which numbers are assigned to letters, digits, and punctuation symbols. Although computers work in ◊binary

ASCII codes

character	binary code	character	binary code
A	1000001	N	1001110
B	1000010	O	1001111
C	1000011	P	1010000
D	1000100	Q	1010001
E	1000101	R	1010010
F	1000110	S	1010011
G	1000111	T	1010100
H	1001000	U	1010101
I	1001001	V	1010110
J	1001010	W	1010111
K	1001011	X	1011000
L	1001100	Y	1011001
M	1001101	Z	1011010

number code, ASCII numbers are usually quoted in decimal or ◊hexadecimal number system numbers. For example, the decimal number 45 (binary 0101101) represents a hyphen, and 65 (binary 1000001) a capital A. The first 32 codes are used for control functions, such as carriage return and backspace.

Strictly speaking, ASCII is a 7-bit binary code, allowing 128 different characters to be represented, but an eighth bit is often used to provide ◊parity or to allow for extra characters. The system is widely used for the storage of text and for the transmission of data between computers.

assembler a program that translates a program written in an assembly language into a complete ◊machine code program that can be executed by a computer. Each instruction in the assembly language is translated into only one machine-code instruction.

assembly language low-level computer-programming language closely related to a computer's internal codes. It consists chiefly of a set of short sequences of letters (mnemonics), which are translated, by a program called an assembler, into ◊machine code for the computer's ◊central processing unit (CPU) to follow directly. In assembly language, for example, 'JMP' means 'jump' and 'LDA' means 'load accumulator'. Assembly code is used by programmers who need to write very fast or efficient programs.

Because they are much easier to use, high-level languages are normally used in preference to assembly languages. An assembly language may still be used in some cases, however, particularly when no suitable high-level language exists or where a very efficient machine-code program is required.

asynchronous irregular or not synchronized. In computer communications, the term is usually applied to data transmitted irregularly rather than as a steady stream. Asynchronous communication uses ◊start bits and ◊stop bits to indicate the beginning and end of each piece of data.

audit trail record of computer operations, showing what has been done and, if available, who has done it. The term is taken from accountancy, but audit trails are now widely used to check many aspects of computer security, in addition to use in accounts programs.

autoexec.bat a file in the ◊MS-DOS operating system that is automatically run when the computer is ◊booted.

AVI (abbreviation for *Audio-Visual Interleave*) file format capable of storing moving images (such as video) with accompanying sound. AVI files can be replayed by any multimedia PC with ◊Windows 3.1 and a ◊soundcard. AVI files are frequently very large (around 50 Mbyte for a five-minute rock video, for example), so they are usually stored on ◊CD-ROM.

B

backing storage memory outside the ◊central processing unit used to store programs and data that are not in current use. Backing storage must be nonvolatile – that is, its contents must not be lost when the power supply to the computer system is disconnected.

backup a copy file that is transferred to another medium, usually a ◊floppy disc or tape. The purpose of this is to have available a copy of a file that can be restored in case of a fault in the system or the file itself. Backup files are also created by many applications (with the extension .BAC or .BAK); a version is therefore available of the original file before it was modified by the current application.

backup system a duplicate computer system that can take over the operation of a main computer system in the event of equipment failure. A large interactive system, such as an airline's ticket-booking system, cannot be out of action for even a few hours without causing considerable disruption. In such cases a complete duplicate computer system may be provided to take over and run the system should the main computer develop a fault or need maintenance.

Backup systems include *incremental backup* and *full backup*.

bandwidth rate of data transmission, measured in ◊bits per second (bps).

bar code pattern of bars and spaces that can be read by a computer. Bar codes are widely used in retailing, industrial distribution, and public libraries. The code is read by a scanning device; the computer determines the code from the widths of the bars and spaces.

BASIC (acronym for *beginner's all-purpose symbolic instruction code*) high-level computer-programming language, developed 1964, originally designed to take advantage of ◊multiuser systems (which can be used by many people at the same time). The language is relatively easy to learn and is popular among microcomputer users.

Most versions make use of an ◊interpreter, which translates BASIC into ◊machine code and allows programs to be entered and run with no intermediate translation. Some more recent versions of BASIC allow a ◊compiler to be used for this process.

batch processing a system for processing data with little or no operator intervention. Batches of data are prepared in advance to be processed during regular 'runs' (for example, each night). This allows efficient use of the computer and is well suited to applications of a repetitive nature, such as a company payroll.

In ◊*interactive computing*, by contrast, data and instructions are entered while the processing program is running.

baud unit that measures the speed of data transmission. One baud represents a transmission rate of one bit per second.

benchmark a measure of the performance of a piece of equipment or software, usually consisting of a standard program or suite of programs. Benchmarks can indicate whether a computer is powerful enough to perform a particular task, and so enable machines to be compared. However, they provide only a very rough guide to practical performance, and may lead manufacturers to design systems that get high scores with the artificial benchmark programs but do not necessarily perform well with day-to-day programs or data.

Benchmark measures include *Whetstones*, *Dhrystones*, *SPECmarks*, and *TPC*. SPECmarks are based on ten programs adopted by the Systems Performance Evaluation Cooperative for benchmarking workstations; the Transaction Processing Performance Council's TPC-B benchmark is used to test databases and on-line systems in banking (debit/credit) environments.

beta version a pre-release version of ◊software or an ◊application program, usually distributed to a limited number of expert users (and often reviewers). Distribution of beta versions allows user testing and feedback to the developer, so that any necessary modifications can be made before release.

Bezier curve curved line invented by Pierre Bézier that connects a series of points (or 'nodes') in the smoothest possible way. The shape of the curve is governed by a series of complex mathematical formulae. They are used in ◊computer graphics and ◊CAD.

Big Blue popular name for ◊IBM, derived from the company's size and its blue logo.

binary number code code based on the binary number system, used to represent instructions and data in all modern digital computers – for example, in the ◊ASCII code system used by most microcomputers, the capital letter A is represented by the binary number 01000001.

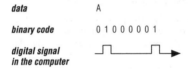

data	A
binary code	0 1 0 0 0 0 0 1
digital signal in the computer	

Because binary numbers use only the digits 0 and 1, they can be represented by any device that can exist in two different states. In a digital computer several different two-state devices are used to store or transmit binary number codes – for example, circuits, which may or may not carry a voltage; discs or tapes, parts of which may or may not be magnetized; and switches, which may be open or closed. Digital computers are designed in this way for two reasons. Firstly, it is much easier and cheaper to construct two-state devices than devices that can exist in more than two states. Secondly, communication between two-state devices is very reliable because only two different signals, 0 or 1 (on or off), need to be recognized.

binary number system system of numbers to base two, using combinations of the digits 1 and 0. Codes based on binary numbers are used to represent instructions and data in all modern digital computers, the values of the binary digits (contracted to 'bits') being stored or transmitted as, for example, open/closed switches, magnetized/ unmagnetized discs and tapes, and high/low voltages in circuits.

The value of any position in a binary number increases by powers of 2 (doubles) with each move from right to left (1, 2, 4, 8, 16, and so on). For example, 1011 in the binary number system means $(1 \times 8) + (0 \times 4) + (1 \times 2) + (1 \times 1)$, which adds up to 11 in the decimal system.

binary search a rapid technique used to find any particular record in a list of records held in sequential order. The computer is programmed to compare the record sought with the record in the middle of the ordered list. This being done, the computer discards the half of the list in which the record does not appear, thereby reducing the number of records left to search by half. This process of selecting the middle record and discarding the unwanted half of the list is repeated until the required record is found.

biological computer proposed technology for computing devices based on growing complex organic molecules (biomolecules) as components. Its theoretical basis is that cells, the building blocks of all living things, have chemical systems that can store and exchange electrons and therefore function as electrical components. It is currently the subject of long-term research.

BIOS (acronym for *basic input/output system*) the part of the ⟡operating system that handles input and output. The term is also used to describe the programs stored in ⟡ROM (and called ROM BIOS), which are automatically run when a computer is switched on allowing it to ⟡boot. BIOS is unaffected by upgrades to the operating system stored on disc.

bistable circuit or *flip-flop* simple electronic circuit that remains in one of two stable states until it receives a pulse (logic 1 signal) through one of its inputs, upon which it switches, or 'flips', over to the other state. Because it is a two-state device, it can be used to store binary digits and is widely used in the ⟡integrated circuits used to build computers.

bit (contraction of *binary digit*) a single binary digit, either 0 or 1. A bit is the smallest unit of data stored in a computer; all other data must be coded into a pattern of individual bits. A ⟡byte represents sufficient computer memory to store a single ⟡character of data, and usually contains eight bits. For example, in the ◊ASCII code system used by most microcomputers the capital letter A would be stored in a single byte of memory as the bit pattern 01000001.

The maximum number of bits that a computer can normally process at once is called a *word*. Microcomputers are often described according to how many bits of information they can handle at once. For instance, the first microprocessor, the Intel 4004 (launched 1971), was a 4-bit device. In the 1970s several different 8-bit computers, many based on the Zilog Z80 or Rockwell 6502 processors, came into common use. During the early 1980s, the IBM personal computer was introduced, using the INTEL 8088 processor, which combined a 16-bit processor with an 8-bit ◊data bus. Business micros of the later 1980s began to use 32-bit processors such as the Intel 80386 and Motorola 68030. Machines based on the first 64-bit microprocessor, the Intel Pentium, appeared 1993.

bit map a pattern of ◊bits used to describe the organization of data. Bit maps are used to store typefaces or graphic images (bit-mapped or ◊raster graphics), with 1 representing black (or a colour) and 0 white.

Bit maps may be used to store a typeface or ◊font, but a separate set of bit maps is required for each typesize. A vector font, by contrast, can be held as one set of data and scaled as required. Bit-mapped graphics are not recommended for images that require scaling (compare ◊vector graphics – those stored in the form of geometric formulas).

bit-mapped font ◊font held in computer memory as sets of bit maps.

bit pad computer input device; see ◊graphics tablet.

block a group of records treated as a complete unit for transfer to or from ◊backing storage. For example, many disc drives transfer data in 512-byte blocks.

Boolean algebra set of algebraic rules, named after mathematician George Boole, in which TRUE and FALSE are equated to 0 and 1. Boolean algebra includes a series of operators (AND, OR, NOT, NAND (NOT AND), NOR, and XOR (exclusive OR)), which can be used to manipulate TRUE and FALSE values (see ◊truth table). It is the basis of computer logic because the truth values can be directly associated with ◊bits. *See table overleaf.*

Boolean algebra: operators

operator	meaning
x AND y	result true if both **x** and **y** are true; otherwise result false
x OR y	result true if either **x** or **y** is true; otherwise result false
x XOR y	result true only if **x** and **y** are different; otherwise result false
NOT y	result true if **x** is false; result false if **x** is true

boot or **bootstrap** the process of starting up a computer. Most computers have a small, built-in boot program that starts automatically when the computer is switched on – its only task is to load a slightly larger program, usually from a hard disc, which in turn loads the main ◊operating system.

In microcomputers the operating system is often held in the permanent ◊ROM memory and the boot program simply triggers its operation.

Some boot programs can be customized so that, for example, the computer, when switched on, always loads and runs a program from a particular backing store or always adopts a particular mode of screen display.

bps (abbreviation for **bits per second**) measure used in specifying data transmission rates.

bridge a device that connects two similar local area networks (LANs). Bridges transfer data in packets between the two networks, without making any changes or interpreting the data in any way. See also ◊router and ◊brouter.

brouter device for connecting computer networks that incorporates the facilities of both a ◊bridge and a ◊router. Brouters usually offer routing over a limited number of ◊protocols, operating by routing where possible and bridging the remaining protocols.

browser any program that allows the user to search for and view data. Browsers are usually limited to a particular type of data, so, for example, a graphics browser will display graphics files stored in many different file formats. Browsers do not permit the user to edit data, but are sometimes able to convert data from one file format to another.

◊Mosaic, a program that allows users to view documents on the ◊World-Wide Web, is an example of a browser.

bubble-jet printer an ◊ink-jet printer in which the ink is heated to boiling point so that it forms a bubble at the end of a nozzle. When the bubble bursts, the ink is transferred to the paper.

bubble memory a memory device based on the creation of small 'bubbles' on a magnetic surface. Bubble memories typically store up to 4 megabits (4 million ◊bits) of information. They are not sensitive to shock and vibration, unlike other memory devices such as disc drives, yet, like magnetic discs, they are nonvolatile and do not lose their information when the computer is switched off.

bubble sort a technique for ◊sorting data. Adjacent items are continually exchanged until the data are in sequence.

buffer a part of the ◊memory used to store data temporarily while it is waiting to be used. For example, a program might store data in a printer buffer until the printer is ready to print it.

bug an ◊error in a program. It can be an error in the logical structure of a program or a syntax error, such as a spelling mistake. Some bugs cause a program to fail immediately; others remain dormant, causing problems only when a particular combination of events occurs. The process of finding and removing errors from a program is called *debugging*.

bulletin board a centre for the electronic storage of messages, usually accessed over the telephone network via ◊electronic mail and a ◊modem. Bulletin boards are usually dedicated to specific interest groups, and may carry messages, notices, and programs.

bus the electrical pathway through which a computer processor communicates with some of its parts and/or peripherals. Physically, a bus is a set of parallel tracks that can carry digital signals; it may take the form of copper tracks laid down on the computer's ◊printed circuit boards, or of an external cable or connection. *See illustration overleaf,*

A computer typically has three internal buses laid down on its main circuit board: a *data bus*, which carries data between the components of the computer; an *address bus*, which selects the route to be followed by any particular data item travelling along the data bus; and a *control*

bus
bus arrangement in a typical microcomputer

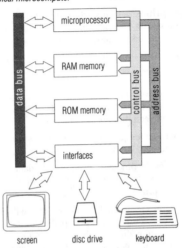

bus, which is used to decide whether data is written to or read from the data bus. An external *expansion bus* is used for linking the computer processor to peripheral devices, such as modems and printers.

byte sufficient computer memory to store a single ◊character of data. The character is stored in the byte of memory as a pattern of ◊bits (binary digits), using a code such as ◊ASCII. A byte usually contains eight bits – for example, the capital letter F can be stored as the bit pattern 01000110.

A single byte can specify 256 values, such as the decimal numbers from 0 to 255; in the case of a single-byte ◊pixel (picture element), it can specify 256 different colours. Three bytes (24 bits) can specify 16,777,216 values. Computer memory size is measured in *kilobytes* (1,024 bytes) or *megabytes* (1,024 kilobytes).

C

C high-level general-purpose computer-programming language popular on minicomputers and microcomputers. Developed in the early 1970s from an earlier language called BCPL, C was first used as the language of the operating system ◊Unix, though it has since become widespread beyond Unix. It is useful for writing fast and efficient systems programs, such as operating systems (which control the operations of the computer).

C++ a high-level programming language used in ◊object-oriented programming. It is derived from the language C.

cache memory a reserved area of the ◊immediate access memory used to increase the running speed of a computer program.

The cache memory may be constructed from ◊SRAM, which is faster but more expensive than the normal ◊DRAM. Most programs access the same instructions or data repeatedly. If these frequently used instructions and data are stored in a fast-access SRAM memory cache, the program will run more quickly. In other cases, the memory cache is normal DRAM, but is used to store frequently used instructions and data that would normally be accessed from ◊backing storage. Access to DRAM is faster than access to backing storage so, again, the program runs more quickly. This type of cache memory is often called a *disc cache*.

CAD (acronym for *computer-aided design*) the use of computers in creating and editing design drawings. CAD also allows such things as automatic testing of designs and multiple or animated three-dimensional views of designs. CAD systems are widely used in architecture, electronics, and engineering, for example in the motor-vehicle industry, where cars designed with the assistance of computers are now commonplace.

A related development is ◊CAM (computer-assisted manufacturing).

Cairo code name for Microsoft's successor to the ◊Windows NT operating system.

CAL (acronym for *computer-assisted learning*) the use of computers in education and training: the computer displays instructional material to a student and then asks questions about the information given; the student's answers determine the sequence of the lessons.

CAM (acronym for *computer-aided manufacturing*) the use of computers to control production processes; in particular, the control of machine tools and ◊robots in factories. In some factories, the whole design and production system has been automated by linking ◊CAD (computer-aided design) to CAM.

Linking flexible CAD/CAM manufacturing to computer-based sales and distribution methods makes it possible to produce semicustomized goods cheaply and in large numbers.

carriage return (CR) in computing, a special code (◊ASCII value 13) that moves the screen cursor or a print head to the beginning of the current line. Most word processors and the ◊MS-DOS operating system use a combination of CR and line feed (LF – ASCII value 10) to represent a hard return. The ◊Unix system, however, uses only LF and therefore files transferred between MS-DOS and Unix require a conversion program.

CCITT abbreviation for ◊*Comité Consultatif International Téléphonique et Télégraphique*, an organization that sets international communications standards.

CD-I (abbreviation for *compact disc-interactive*) compact disc developed by Philips for storing a combination of video, audio, text, and pictures. It is intended principally for the consumer market to be used in systems using a combination of computer and television. An alternative format is ◊DVI (digital video interactive).

CD-R (abbreviation for *compact disc-recordable*) compact disc on which data can be overwritten (compare ◊CD-ROM, compact disc read-only memory). The disc combines magnetic and optical technology: during the writing process, a laser melts the surface of the disc, thereby allowing the magnetic elements of the surface layer to be realigned.

CD-ROM (abbreviation for *compact-disc read-only memory*) computer storage device developed from the technology of the audio ◊compact disc. It consists of a plastic-coated metal disc, on which binary digital information is etched in the form of microscopic pits. This can then be read optically by passing a light beam over the disc. CD-ROMs typically hold about 550 ◊megabytes of data, and are used in distributing large amounts of text and graphics, such as encyclopedias, catalogues, and technical manuals.

Standard CD-ROMs cannot have information written onto them by computer, but must be manufactured from a master. Although recordable CDs, called CD-R discs, have been developed for use as computer discs, they are as yet too expensive for widespread use. A compact disc that can be overwritten repeatedly by a computer has also been developed; see ◊optical disc. The compact disc, with its enormous storage capability, may eventually replace the magnetic disc as the most common form of backing store for computers.

The technology is being developed rapidly: a standard CD-ROM disc spins at between 240–1170 rpm, but faster discs have been introduced which speed up data retrieval and research is being conducted into using multiple layers on the surface of the disc to enable much larger quantities of data to be stored on a single disc.

PhotoCD, developed by Kodak and released in 1992, transfers ordinary still photographs onto CD-ROM discs.

CD-ROM drive a disc drive for reading CD-ROM discs. The vast majority of CD-ROM drives conform to the Yellow Book standard, defined by Philips and Sony. Because of this, all drives are essentially interchangeable. CD-ROM drives are available either as stand-alone or built-in units with a variety of interfaces (connections) and access times.

CD-ROM XA (CD-ROM extended *a*rchitecture) a set of standards for storing multimedia information on CD-ROM. Developed by Philips,

Sony, and Microsoft, it is a partial development of the ◊CD-I standard. It interleaves data (as in CD-I) so that blocks of audio data are sandwiched between blocks of text, graphics, or video. This allows parallel streams of data to be handled, so that information can be seen and heard simultaneously. Unlike CD-I, CD-ROM XA discs are playable on any ◊CD-ROM drive with an appropriate interface.

CDTV (abbreviation for *Commodore Dynamic Total Vision*) multimedia computer system developed by Commodore. It is designed for the home and is a direct rival to ◊CD-I. It consists of a box about the size of a home video recorder, containing an Amiga 500 computer and a ◊CD-ROM drive. CDTV discs can store a combination of text, pictures, sound, and video. Like CD-I, CDTV plugs into a TV set and stereo system. CDTV cannot play CD-ROM or CD-I discs.

central processing unit (CPU) main component of a computer, the part that executes individual program instructions and controls the operation of other parts. It is sometimes called the central processor or, when contained on a single integrated circuit, a microprocessor.

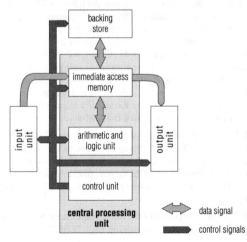

The CPU has three main components: the ***arithmetic and logic unit*** (ALU), where all calculations and logical operations are carried out; a ***control unit***, which decodes, synchronizes, and executes program instruction; and the ***immediate access memory***, which stores the data and programs on which the computer is currently working. All these components contain ◊registers, which are memory locations reserved for specific purposes.

These registers include the ◊accumulator, the ◊instruction register, and the ◊sequence-control register.

Centronics interface standard type of computer ◊interface, used to connect computers to ◊parallel devices, usually printers. (Centronics was an important printer manufacturer in the early days of micro-computing.)

CGA (abbreviation for ***colour graphics adapter***) first colour display system for IBM PCs and compatible machines. It has been superseded by ◊EGA, ◊VGA, ◊SVGA, and ◊XGA.

character one of the symbols that can be represented in a computer. Characters include letters, numbers, spaces, punctuation marks, and special symbols.

character printer computer ◊printer that prints one character at a time.

character set the complete set of symbols that can be used in a program or recognized by a computer. It may include letters, digits, spaces, punctuation marks, and special symbols.

character type check in computing, a ◊validation check to ensure that an input data item does not contain invalid characters. For example, an input name may be checked to ensure that it contains only letters of the alphabet or an input six-figure date may be checked to ensure it contains only numbers.

check digit a digit attached to an important code number as a ◊validation check.

checksum a ◊control total of specific items of data. A checksum is used as a check that data have been input or transmitted correctly. It is used in communications and in, for example, accounts programs. See also ◊validation.

Chicago code name for ◊Windows 95, the successor to Windows 3.1.

chip or *silicon chip* another name for an *◊integrated circuit*, a complete electronic circuit on a slice of silicon (or other semiconductor) crystal only a few millimetres square.

CISC (acronym for *complex instruction set computer*) a microprocessor (processor on a single chip) that can carry out a large number of ◊machine code instructions – for example, the Intel 80386. The term was introduced to distinguish them from the more rapid ◊RISC (reduced instruction set computer) processors, which handle only a smaller set of instructions.

click to press down and then immediately release a button on a ◊mouse. The phrase 'to click on' means to select an ◊icon on a computer screen by moving the mouse cursor to the icon's position and clicking a mouse button. See also ◊double click.

client–server architecture computing system in which the mechanics of looking after data are separated from the programs that use the data. For example, the 'server' might be a central database, typically located on a large computer that is reserved for this purpose. The 'client' would be an ordinary program that requests data from the server as needed.

clipboard a temporary file or memory area where data can be stored before being copied into an application file. It is used, for example, in cut-and-paste operations.

clock interrupt an ◊interrupt signal generated by the computer's internal electronic clock.

clock rate the frequency of a computer's internal electronic clock. Every computer contains an electronic clock, which produces a sequence of regular electrical pulses used by the control unit to synchronize the components of the computer and regulate the ◊fetch–execute cycle by which program instructions are processed.

A fixed number of time pulses is required in order to execute each particular instruction. The speed at which a computer can process instructions therefore depends on the clock rate: increasing the clock rate will decrease the time required to complete each particular instruction.

Clock rates are measured in *megahertz* (MHz), or millions of pulses a second. Microcomputers commonly have a clock rate of 8–50 MHz.

CMOS (abbreviation for *complementary metal-oxide semiconductor*) family of integrated circuits (chips) widely used in building electronic systems.

CMYK (abbreviation for *cyan–magenta–yellow–black*) four-colour separation used in most (subtractive) colour printing processes. Representation on computer screens normally uses the additive ◊RGB method and so conversion is usually necessary on output for printing either on colour printers or as separations.

CNC abbreviation for ◊*computer numerical control*.

coaxial cable electric cable that consists of a solid or stranded central conductor insulated from and surrounded by a solid or braided conducting tube or sheath. It can transmit the high-frequency signals used in television, telephone, and other telecommunications transmissions.

COBOL (acronym for *common business-oriented language*) high-level computer-programming language, designed in the late 1950s for commercial data-processing problems; it has become the major language in this field. COBOL features powerful facilities for file handling and business arithmetic. Program instructions written in this language make extensive use of words and look very much like English sentences. This makes COBOL one of the easiest languages to learn and understand.

COM acronym for ◊*computer output on microfilm/microfiche*.

Comité Consultatif International Téléphonique et Télégraphique (CCITT) international organization that determines international communications standards and protocols for data communications, including ◊fax.

command language a set of commands and the rules governing their use, by which users control a program. For example, an

◊operating system may have commands such as SAVE and DELETE, or a payroll program may have commands for adding and amending staff records.

command line interface (CLI) a character-based interface in which a prompt is displayed on the screen at which the user types a command, followed by ◊carriage return, at which point the command, if valid, is executed.

compact disc (or *CD*) disc for storing digital information, about 12 cm/4.5 in across, mainly used for music, when it can have over an hour's playing time. The compact disc is made of aluminium with a transparent plastic coating; the metal disc underneath is etched by a laser beam with microscopic pits that carry a digital code representing the sounds. During playback, a laser beam reads the code and produces signals that are changed into near-exact replicas of the original sounds.

CD-ROM, or *Compact-Disc Read-Only Memory*, is used to store written text, pictures, and video clips in addition to music. The discs are ideal for large works, such as catalogues and encyclopedias.

CD-I, or *Compact-Disc Interactive*, is a form of CD-ROM used with a computerized reader, which responds intelligently to the user's instructions.

Recordable CDs, called *WORM*s ('write once, read many times'), are used as computer discs, but are as yet too expensive for home use.

*Video CD*s, on sale 1994, store an hour of video. High-density video discs, first publicly demonstrated 1995, can hold full-length features.

Erasable CDs, which can be erased and recorded many times, are also used by the computer industry. These are coated with a compound of cobalt and gadolinium, which alters the polarization of light falling on it. In the reader, the light reflected from the disc is passed through polarizing filters and the changes in polarization are converted into electrical signals.

See feature article overleaf.

compiler computer program that translates programs written in a ◊high-level language into machine code (the form in which they can be run by the computer). The compiler translates each high-level instruction into several machine-code instructions – in a process called

compiler
flowchart showing how a compiler works

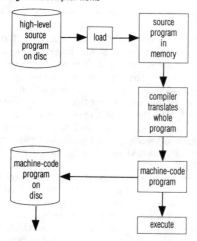

compilation – and produces a complete independent program that can be run by the computer as often as required, without the original source program being present.

Different compilers are needed for different high-level languages and for different computers. In contrast to using an ◊interpreter, using a compiler adds slightly to the time needed to develop a new program because the machine- code program must be recompiled after each change or correction. Once compiled, however, the machine-code program will run much faster than an interpreted program.

complementary metal-oxide semiconductor (CMOS) in electronics, a particular way of manufacturing integrated circuits (chips). The main advantage of CMOS chips is their low power requirement and heat dissipation, which enables them to be used in electronic watches and portable microcomputers. However, CMOS circuits are

The CD shows its versatility

The compact disc (CD) is one of the most successful 'formats' ever invented. The 5-inch silver disc in its clear jewel case looks attractive, is easy to store and handle, performs well, seems not to deteriorate, and very rarely goes wrong. It thus commands a premium price over audio cassettes and VHS video cassettes, which are less attractive, more awkward to assemble and, because of their thin tape and complex plastic parts, prone to fail. Now the CD format is being extended into other areas. As well as hi-fi sound, CDs can also be used for computer programs, text, graphics, speech, animation, photographic images, and even full-screen, full-motion video (FMV for short) with a quality that compares with VHS.

CDs are already an important form of computer storage with products on CD-ROM (read-only memory). One CD can hold about 550 megabytes of data or about 90 million words of text. This is easily enough to hold a very large encyclopedia, a year's issues of a newspaper, several years' issues of most journals, or hundreds of novels. Obviously the cost of pressing a CD – now less than 50p – is far less than the cost of producing the paper equivalents. And the CD is more powerful, since you can search in seconds for, say, every York Road in the country.

But a CD is not limited to holding numbers or text. The electronic edition of *The Hutchinson Encyclopedia* is a good example of a so-called 'multimedia' disc. With a PC that runs Windows, you have access not only to 1.8 million words of text but also to over 2,000 pictures, tables, maps, and accompanying sound sequences. If, for instance, you were to look up the entry for Martin Luther King, you would be able to read his biography, browse through pictures of his life and times, then listen to his famous 'I have a dream' speech.

Volume production has brought down the prices of drives and discs, and standards have been established for IBM PC-compatible computers by the Multimedia PC Council, so this kind of thing is becoming popular. Of course it is still not quite a mass market, but there are other plans to promote the use of CDs in the home. The most important are CD-I and PhotoCD.

CD-I (for compact disc-interactive) is a new format launched in the UK in May 1992 with the backing of Philips, Sony, Matsushita, and other consumer electronics firms. CD-I extends the CD-ROM format by providing for interleaved sound and graphics, and later it will be expanded to include FMV. (Buyers of the early players will be offered an upgrade cartridge to plug into their machines.)

Most CD-I discs are classified as 'edutainment', and half of the first 32 titles launched in the UK were aimed at children. These include stories, paint programs and Sesame Street. PhotoCD, a CD-I-compatible format developed by Kodak and Philips, puts 35 mm snapshots onto CDs as a sort of high-quality 'digital negative'. Not only can you display your snaps on TV, you can zoom in on selected parts, crop, recolour, and otherwise manipulate them.

CD-I and PhotoCD players look like an ordinary CD players, and also play CD-DA (standard Digital Audio) discs. The fact that the CD-I or PhotoCD player includes a powerful microcomputer with a real-time operating system – something like an Apple Macintosh or Commodore Amiga – is nowhere mentioned in the promotional literature. But computer and video games suppliers can achieve similar effects by adding CD drives to their machines, rather than by adding computers to their players. Early examples of this approach include Fujitsu's FM-Towns computer, NEC's PC Engine games console, and Commodore's Amiga-based CDTV system. Nintendo and Sega entered this market 1992.

For gamers, CDs have huge benefits in removing the space restrictions that limit the use of high-quality sound and graphics. Instead of being limited to one or two megabytes of code, authors will be able to use about five hundred. Piracy will be less of a problem too, and users won't have to worry about fragile floppy discs being damaged or corrupted.

Twelve years ago, when the compact disc was launched, it seemed expensive and of limited appeal. The new CD-I format might seem that way too, today, but in the next decade it promises to become even more ubiquitous. Indeed, Motorola is already planning to put all the CD-I electronics on a single microchip, making the additional cost marginal. CD-I machines will then completely replace CD players for all but a few audiophiles.

expensive to manufacture and have lower operating speeds than have circuits of the ◊transistor–transistor logic (TTL) family.

CompuServe large (US-based) public on-line data service. It is widely used for ◊electronic mail and ◊bulletin boards.

It is easier to use than the Internet and most computer hardware and software suppliers provide support for their products on CompuServe. Worldwide subscribers to CompuServe have risen from half a million 1988 to nearly 2 million 1994.

computer programmable electronic device that processes data and performs calculations and other symbol-manipulation tasks. There are three types: the ◊*digital computer*, which manipulates information coded as binary numbers (see ◊binary number system); the ◊*analogue computer*, which works with continuously varying quantities; and the *hybrid computer*, which has characteristics of both analogue and digital computers.

There are four types of digital computer, corresponding roughly to their size and intended use. *Microcomputers* are the smallest and most common, used in small businesses, at home, and in schools. They are usually single-user machines. *Minicomputers* are found in medium-sized businesses and university departments. They may support from 10 to 200 or so users at once. *Mainframes*, which can often service several hundred users simultaneously, are found in large organizations, such as national companies and government departments. *Super-computers* are mostly used for highly complex scientific tasks, such as analysing the results of nuclear physics experiments and weather forecasting. Microcomputers now come in a range of sizes from battery-powered pocket PCs and electronic organizers, notebook and laptop PCs to floor-standing tower systems that may serve local area ◊networks or work as minicomputers. Indeed, most minicomputers are now built using low-cost microprocessors, and large-scale computers built out of multiple microprocessors are starting to challenge traditional mainframe and supercomputer designs.

history Computers are only one of the many kinds of computing device. The first mechanical computer was conceived by Charles Babbage 1835, but it never went beyond the design stage. In 1943,

computer
typical mainframe computer system

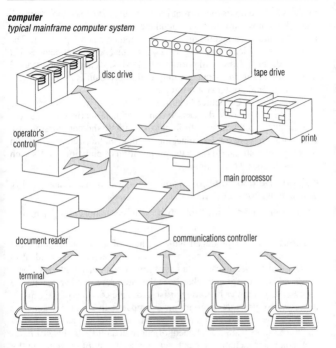

more than a century later, Thomas Flowers built Colossus, the first electronic computer. Working with him at the time was Alan Turing, a mathematician who seven years earlier had published a paper on the theory of computing machines that had a major impact on subsequent developments. John Von Neumann's computer, EDVAC, built 1949, was the first to use binary arithmetic and to store its operating instructions internally. This design still forms the basis of today's computers.
basic components At the heart of a computer is the ◊central processing unit (CPU), which performs all the computations. This is supported by

memory, which holds the current program and data, and 'logic arrays', which help move information around the system. A main power supply is needed and, for a mainframe or minicomputer, a cooling system. The computer's 'device driver' circuits control the ◊peripheral devices that can be attached. These will normally be keyboards and ◊VDUs (visual display units) for user input and output, disc drive units for mass memory storage, and printers for printed output.

Under the UK Computer Misuse Act 1990 three new offences were introduced: unauthorized access to computer material (ie. out of curiosity), unauthorized access with intent to facilitate the commission of a crime (for example fraud or blackmail), and unauthorized modification of computer material (to deter the propagation of malicious codes such as ◊viruses and ◊Trojan horses).

computer-aided design use of computers to create and modify design drawings; see ◊CAD.

computer-aided manufacturing use of computers to regulate production processes in industry; see ◊CAM.

computer art art produced with the help of a computer. Since the 1950s the aesthetic use of computers has been increasingly evident in most artistic disciplines, including film animation, architecture, and music. ◊Computer graphics has been the most developed area, with the 'paint-box' computer liberating artists from the confines of the canvas. It is now also possible to programme computers in advance to generate graphics, music, and sculpture, according to 'instructions' which may include a preprogrammed element of unpredictability. In this last function, computer technology has been seen as a way of challenging the elitist nature of art by putting artistic creativity within relatively easy reach of anyone owning a computer.

computer-assisted learning use of computers in education and training; see ◊CAL.

computer engineer job classification for ◊computer personnel. A computer engineer repairs and maintains computer hardware.

computer game or *video game* any computer-controlled game in which the computer (sometimes) opposes the human player. Computer games typically employ fast, animated graphics on a ◊VDU (visual display unit), and synthesized sound.

Commercial computer games became possible with the advent of the ◊microprocessor in the mid-1970s and rapidly became popular as amusement-arcade games, using dedicated chips. Available games range from chess to fighter-plane simulations.

computer generation any of the five broad groups into which computers may be classified: ***first generation*** the earliest computers, developed in the 1940s and 1950s, made from valves and wire circuits; ***second generation*** from the early 1960s, based on transistors and printed circuits; ***third generation*** from the late 1960s, using integrated circuits and often sold as families of computers, such as the IBM 360 series; ***fourth generation*** using ◊microprocessors, large-scale integration (LSI), and sophisticated programming languages, still in use in the 1990s; and ***fifth generation*** based on parallel processing and very large-scale integration, currently under development.

computer graphics use of computers to display and manipulate information in pictorial form. Input may be achieved by scanning an image, by drawing with a mouse or stylus on a graphics tablet, or by drawing directly on the screen with a light pen.

The output may be as simple as a pie chart, or as complex as an animated sequence in a science-fiction film (see also ◊morphing), or a seemingly three-dimensional engineering blueprint. The drawing is stored in the computer as ◊raster graphics or ◊vector graphics. Computer graphics are increasingly used in computer-aided design (◊CAD), and to generate models and simulations in engineering, meteorology, medicine and surgery, and other fields of science.

Recent developments in software mean that designers on opposite sides of the world will soon be able to work on complex three-dimensional computer models using ordinary PCs linked by telephone lines rather then powerful graphics workstations.

computer literacy ability to understand and make use of computer technology in an everyday context.

computer numerical control control of machine tools, most often milling machines, by a computer. The pattern of work for the machine to follow, which often involves performing repeated sequences of actions, is described using a special-purpose programming language.

computer operator job classification for ◊computer personnel. Computer operators work directly with the computer, running the programs, changing discs and tapes, loading paper into printers, and ensuring all ◊data security procedures are followed.

computer output on microfilm/microfiche (COM) technique for producing computer output in very compact, photographically reduced form (◊microform).

computer personnel people who work with or are associated with computers. In a large computer department the staff may work under the direction of a *data processing manager*, who supervises and coordinates the work performed. Computer personnel can be broadly divided into two categories: those who run and maintain existing ◊applications programs (programs that perform a task for the benefit of the user) and those who develop new applications.

Personnel who run existing applications programs: *data control staff* receive information from computer users (for instance, from the company's wages clerks), ensure that it is processed as required, and return it to them in processed form; *data preparation staff*, or *keyboard operators*, prepare the information received by the data control staff so that it is ready for processing by computer. Once the information has been typed at the keyboard of a VDU (or at a ◊key-to-disc system or key-to-tape station), it is placed directly onto a medium such as disc or tape; *computer operators* work directly with computers, running the programs, changing discs and tapes, loading paper into printers, and ensuring that all ◊data security procedures are followed; *computer engineers* repair and maintain computer hardware; *file librarians*, or *media librarians*, store and issue the data files used by the department; an *operations manager* coordinates all the day-to-day activities of these staff. Personnel who develop new applications: *systems analysts* carry out the analysis of an existing system (see ◊systems analysis), whether already computerized or not, and prepare proposals for a new system; *programmers* write the software needed for new systems.

computer program coded instructions for a computer; see ◊program.

computer simulation representation of a real-life situation in a computer program. For example, the program might simulate the flow of customers arriving at a bank. The user can alter variables, such as the number of cashiers on duty, and see the effect.

More complex simulations can model the behaviour of chemical reactions or even nuclear explosions. The behaviour of solids and liquids at high temperatures can be simulated using quantum simulation. Computers also control the actions of machines – for example, a flight simulator models the behaviour of real aircraft and allows training to take place in safety. Computer simulations are very useful when it is too dangerous, time consuming, or simply impossible to carry out a real experiment or test.

computer terminal the device whereby the operator communicates with the computer; see ◊terminal.

config.sys the ◊configuration file used by the MS-DOS and OS/2 ◊operating systems. It is read when the system is ◊booted.

configuration the way in which a system, whether it be ◊hardware and/or ◊software, is set up. A minimum configuration is often referred to for a particular application, and this will usually include a specification of processor, disc and memory size, and peripherals required.

console a combination of keyboard and screen (also described as a terminal). For a multiuser system, such as ◊Unix, there is only one system console from which the system can be administered, while there may be many user terminals. See also ◊games console.

control bus the electrical pathway, or ◊bus, used to communicate control signals.

control character any character produced by depressing the control key (Ctrl) on a keyboard at the same time as another (usually alphabetical) key. The control characters form the first 32 ◊ASCII characters and most have specific meanings according to the operating system used. They are also used in combination to provide formatting control in many word processors, although the user may not enter them explicitly.

control total a ◊validation check in which an arithmetic total of a specific field from a group of records is calculated. This total is input together with the data to which it refers. The program recalculates the control total and compares it with the one entered to ensure that no entry errors have been made.

control unit the component of the ◊central processing unit that decodes, synchronizes, and executes program instructions.

coprocessor an additional ◊processor that works with the main ◊central processing unit to carry out a specific function. The two most common coprocessors are the *mathematical coprocessor*, used to speed up calculations, and the *graphic coprocessor*, used to improve the handling of graphics.

copy protection techniques used to prevent illegal copying of computer programs. Copy protection is not used as frequently as it used to be because it also prevents legal copying (for backup purposes). Alternative techniques to prevent illegal use include ◊dongles, passwords and the need to uninstall a program before it can be installed on another machine.

corruption of data introduction or presence of errors in data. Most computers use a range of ◊verification and ◊validation routines to prevent corrupt data from entering the computer system or detect corrupt data that are already present.

CP/M (abbreviation for *control program/monitor* or *control program for microcomputers*) one of the earliest ◊operating systems for microcomputers. It was written by Gary Kildall, who founded Digital Research, and became a standard for microcomputers based on the Intel 8080 and Zilog Z80 8-bit microprocessors. In the 1980s it was superseded by Microsoft's ◊MS-DOS, written for 16-bit microprocessors.

CPU abbreviation for ◊*central processing unit*.

Cray Seymour Roger 1925– . US computer scientist and pioneer in the field of supercomputing. He designed one of the earliest computers to contain transistors 1960. In 1972 he formed Cray Research to build the first ◊supercomputer, the Cray-1, released 1976. Its success led to the production of further supercomputers, including the Cray-2 1985, the Cray Y-MP (a multiprocessor design)1988, and the Cray-3 1989.

critical path analysis procedure used in the management of complex projects to minimize the amount of time taken. The analysis shows which subprojects can run in parallel with each other, and which have to be completed before other subprojects can follow on.

By identifying the time required for each separate subproject and the relationship between the subprojects, it is possible to produce a planning schedule showing when each subproject should be started and finished in order to complete the whole project most efficiently. Complex projects may involve hundreds of subprojects, and computer ◊applications packages for critical path analysis are widely used to help reduce the time and effort involved in their analysis.

CUA (abbreviation for *common user access*) standard designed by ◊Microsoft to ensure that identical actions, such as saving a file or accessing help, can be carried out using the same keystrokes in any piece of software. For example, in programs written to the CUA standard, help is always summoned by pressing the F1 function key. New programs should be easier to use because users will not have to learn new commands to perform standard tasks.

cursor on a computer screen, the symbol that indicates the current entry position (where the next character will appear). It usually consists of a solid rectangle or underline character, flashing on and off.

cyberspace the imaginary, interactive 'worlds' created by computers; often used interchangeably with 'virtual world' or ◊'virtual reality'. The invention of the word 'cyberspace' is generally credited to US science-fiction writer William Gibson (1948–   ) and his first novel *Neuromancer* 1984.

As well as meaning the interactive environment encountered in a virtual reality system, cyberspace is 'where' the global community of computer-linked individuals and groups lives. From the mid-1980s, the development of computer networks and telecommunications, both international (such as the ◊Internet) and local (such as the services known as 'bulletin board' or conferencing systems), made possible the instant exchange of messages using ◊electronic mail and electronic conferencing systems directly from the individual's own home.

cylinder combination of the tracks on all the platters making up a fixed disc that can be accessed without moving the read/write heads.

D

DAC abbreviation for ◊ *digital-to-analogue converter*.

daisywheel printing head in a computer printer or typewriter that consists of a small plastic or metal disc made up of many spokes (like the petals of a daisy). At the end of each spoke is a character in relief. The daisywheel is rotated until the spoke bearing the required character is facing an inked ribbon, then a hammer strikes the spoke against the ribbon, leaving the impression of the character on the paper beneath.

The daisywheel can be changed to provide different typefaces; however, daisywheel printers cannot print graphics nor can they print more than one typeface in the same document. For these reasons, they are rapidly becoming obsolete.

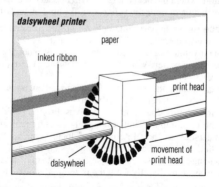

DARPAnet early US computer network; see ◊ARPAnet.

data facts, figures, and symbols, especially as stored in computers. The term is often used to mean raw, unprocessed facts, as distinct from information, to which a meaning or interpretation has been applied.

database a structured collection of data, which may be manipulated to select and sort desired items of information. For example, an accounting system might be built around a database containing details of customers and suppliers. In larger computers, the database makes data available to the various programs that need it, without the need for those programs to be aware of how the data are stored. The term is also sometimes used for simple record-keeping systems, such as mailing lists, in which there are facilities for searching, sorting, and producing records.

There are three main types (or 'models'): hierarchical, network, and ◊relational database, of which relational is the most widely used. A *free-text database* is one that holds the unstructured text of articles or books in a form that permits rapid searching.

A collection of databases is known as a *databank*. A database-man-agement system (DBMS) program ensures that the integrity of the data is maintained by controlling the degree of access of the ◊applications programs using the data. Databases are normally used by large organi-zations with mainframes or minicomputers.

A telephone directory stored as a database might allow all the people whose names start with the letter B to be selected by one program, and all those living in Chicago by another.

data bus the electrical pathway, or ◊bus, used to carry data between the components of the computer.

data capture collecting information for computer processing and analysis. Data may be captured automatically – for example, by a ◊sensor that continuously monitors physical conditions such as temper-ature – or manually; for example, by reading electricity meters.

data communications sending and receiving data via any commu-nications medium, such as a telephone line. The term usually implies that the data are digital (such as computer data) rather than analogue (such as voice messages). However, in the ISDN (◊Integrated Services Digital Network) system, all data – including voices and video images – are transmitted digitally.

data compression techniques for reducing the amount of storage needed for a given amount of data. They include word tokenization (in which frequently used words are stored as shorter codes), variable bit lengths (in which common characters are represented by fewer ♭bits than less common ones), and run-length encoding (in which a repeated value is stored once along with a count).

In *lossless compression* the original file is retrieved unchanged after decompression. Some types of data (sound and pictures) can be stored by *lossy compression* where some detail is lost during compression, but the loss is not noticeable. Lossy compression allows a greater level of compression.

data control staff job classification for ♭computer personnel. Data control staff receive information from computer users, ensure that it is processed as required, and return it to them in processed form.

data dictionary a file that holds data about data – for example, lists of files, number of records in each file, and types of fields. Data dictionaries are used by database software to enable access to the data; they are not normally accessible to the user.

data flow chart diagram illustrating the possible routes that data can take through a system or program; see ♭flow chart.

data input entering data into a computer system.

data logging the process, usually automatic, of capturing and recording a sequence of values for later processing and analysis by computer. For example, the level in a water-storage tank might be automatically logged every hour over a seven-day period, so that a computer could produce an analysis of water use.

data preparation preparing data for computer input by transferring it to a machine-readable medium. This usually involves typing the data at a keyboard (or at a ♭key-to-disc or key-to-tape station) so that it can be transferred directly to tapes or discs. Various methods of direct data capture, such as ♭bar codes, ♭optical mark recognition (OMR), and ♭optical character recognition (OCR), have been developed to reduce or eliminate lengthy data preparation before computer input.

data preparation staff job classification for ◊computer personnel. Data preparation staff prepare information so that it is ready for processing by computer. This often entails typing the data at a keyboard so that it can be transferred to a computer medium (see ◊media) like disc or tape.

data processing (DP) use of computers for performing clerical tasks such as stock control, payroll, and dealing with orders. DP systems are typically ◊batch processing systems, running on mainframe computers. DP is sometimes called EDP (electronic data processing).

A large organization usually has a special department to support its DP activities, which might include the writing and maintenance of software (programs), control and operation of the computers, and an analysis of the organization's information requirements.

See also ◊computer personnel.

data processing manager job classification for ◊computer personnel. A data processing manager supervises and coordinates the work of the computer department.

data protection safeguarding of information about individuals stored on computers, to protect privacy.

The Council of Europe adopted, in 1981, a Data Protection Convention, which led in the UK to the Data Protection Act 1984. This requires computer databases containing personal information to be registered, and users to process only accurate information and to retain the information only for a necessary period and for specified purposes. Subject to certain exemptions, individuals have a right of access to their personal data and to have any errors corrected.

Data Protection Act UK Act of Parliament 1984 that gave the right to a copy of personal information held on computer files and to have inaccurate information corrected or erased. Individuals can complain to the Data Protection Registrar if the provisions of the Act have been broken and can claim compensation from the courts if damaged by inaccurate information or by the loss, unauthorized destruction, or disclosure of that information.

data security precautions taken to prevent the loss or misuse of data, whether accidental or deliberate. These include measures that ensure

data security
one method of write protection

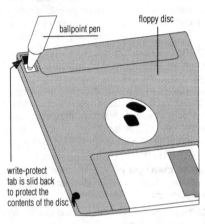

ballpoint pen

floppy disc

write-protect
tab is slid back
to protect the
contents of the disc

that only authorized personnel can gain entry to a computer system or file, and regular procedures for storing and 'backing up' data, which enable files to be retrieved or recreated in the event of loss, theft, or damage.

A number of ◊verification and ◊validation techniques may also be used to prevent data from being lost or corrupted by misprocessing:

Encryption involves the translation of data into a form that is meaningless to unauthorized users who do not have the necessary decoding software.

Passwords can be chosen by, or issued to, individual users. These secret words (or combinations of alphanumeric characters) may have to be entered each time a user logs on to a computer system or attempts to access a particular protected file.

Physical access to the computer facilities can be restricted by locking entry doors and storage cabinets.

Master files (files that are updated periodically) can be protected by storing successive versions, or *generations*, of these files and of the transaction files used to update them. The most recent version of the master file may then be recreated, if necessary, from a previous generation. It is common practice to store the three most recent versions of a master file (often called the grandfather, father, and son generations).

Direct-access files are protected by making regular *dumps*, or back-up copies. Because the individual records in direct-access files are constantly being accessed and updated, specific generations of these files cannot be said to exist. The files are therefore dumped at fixed time intervals onto a secure form of backing store. A record, or log, is also kept of all the changes made to a file between security dumps.

Fireproof safes are used to store file generations or sets of security dumps, so that the system can be restarted on a new computer in the event of a fire in the computer department.

Write-protect mechanisms on discs or tapes allow data to be read but not deleted, altered, or overwritten. For example, the protective case of a 3½-inch floppy disc has a write-protect tab that can be slid back with the tip of a pencil or pen to protect the disc's contents.

data terminator or *rogue value* a special value used to mark the end of a list of input data items. The computer must be able to detect that the data terminator is different from the input data in some way – for instance, a negative number might be used to signal the end of a list of positive numbers, or 'XXX' might be used to terminate the entry of a list of names.

dBASE family of microcomputer programs used for manipulating large quantities of data; also, a related ◊fourth-generation language. The first version, dBASE II, appeared in 1981; it has since become the basis for a recognized standard for database applications, known as Xbase.

DDE the abbreviation for ◊*dynamic data exchange*, a form of communication between processes used in Microsoft Windows.

debugging finding and removing errors, or ◊bugs, from a computer program or system.

DEC (abbreviation for *Digital Equipment Corporation*) US computer manufacturer. DEC was founded by US computer scientists Kenneth

Olsen and Harlan Anderson, and was the first ◊minicomputer manufacturer. It became the world's second largest computer manufacturer, after ◊IBM, but made huge losses in the early 1990s. DEC's most successful computers were the PDP-11 and the VAX. The former was used in the creation of the ◊Unix operating system.

decimal number system or *denary number system* the most commonly used number system, to the base ten. Decimal numbers do not necessarily contain a decimal point; 563, 5.63, and –563 are all decimal numbers. Other systems include the ◊binary number system, ◊octal number system, and ◊hexadecimal number system.

Decimal numbers may be thought of as written under column headings based on the number ten. For example, the number 2,567 stands for:

1,000s	*100s*	*10s*	*1s*
(10^3)	(10^2)	(10^1)	(10^0)
2	5	6	7

Large decimal numbers may also be expressed in ◊floating-point notation.

decision table a method of describing a procedure for a program to follow, based on comparing possible decisions and their consequences. It is often used as an aid in systems design.

The top part of the table contains the conditions for making decisions (for example, if a number is negative rather than positive and is less than 1), and the bottom part describes the outcomes when those conditions are met. The program either ends or repeats the operation.

declarative programming computer programming that does not describe how to solve a problem, but rather describes the logical structure of the problem. It is used in the programming language PROLOG. Running such a program is more like proving an assertion than following a ◊procedure.

decoder an electronic circuit used to select one of several possible data pathways. Decoders are, for example, used to direct data to individual memory locations within a computer's immediate access memory.

dedicated computer computer built into another device for the purpose of controlling or supplying information to it. Its use has increased dramatically since the advent of the ♭microprocessor: washing machines, digital watches, cars, and video recorders all now have their own processors.

A dedicated system is a general-purpose computer system confined to performing only one function for reasons of efficiency or convenience. A word processor is an example.

defragmentation program or *disc optimizer* a program that rearranges data on disc so that files are not scattered in many small sections. See also ♭fragmentation.

delete remove or erase. In computing, the deletion of a character removes it from the file; the deletion of a file normally means removing its directory entry, rather than actually deleting it from the disc. Many systems now have an ♭undelete facility that allows the restoration of the directory entry. While deleted files may not have been removed from the disc, they can be overwritten.

desktop a graphical representation of file systems, in which applications and files are represented by pictures (icons), which can be triggered by a single or double click with a ♭mouse button. Such a ♭graphical user interface can be compared with the ♭command line interface, which is character-based.

desktop publishing (DTP) use of microcomputers for small-scale typesetting and page makeup. DTP systems are capable of producing camera-ready pages (pages ready for photographing and printing), made up of text and graphics, with text set in different typefaces and sizes. The page can be previewed on the screen before final printing on a laser printer.

DIANE (acronym for *direct information access network for Europe*) collection of information suppliers, or 'hosts', for the European computer network.

digit any of the numbers from 0 to 9 in the decimal system. Different bases have different ranges of digits. For example, the ♭hexadecimal number system has digits 0 to 9 and A to F, whereas the binary system has two digits (or ♭bits), 0 and 1.

digital in electronics and computing, a term meaning 'coded as numbers'. A digital system uses two-state, either on/off or high/low voltage pulses, to encode, receive, and transmit information. A *digital display* shows discrete values as numbers (as opposed to an analogue signal, such as the continuous sweep of a pointer on a dial).

Digital electronics is the technology that underlies digital techniques. Low-power, miniature, integrated circuits (chips) provide the means for the coding, storage, transmission, processing, and reconstruction of information of all kinds.

digital audio tape (DAT) digitally recorded audio tape produced in cassettes that can carry two hours of sound on each side and are about half the size of standard cassettes. DAT players/recorders were developed 1987 but not marketed in the UK until 1989. Prerecorded cassettes are copy-protected. The first DAT for computer data was introduced 1988.

DAT machines are constructed like video cassette recorders (though they use metal audio tape), with a movable playback head, the tape winding in a spiral around a rotating drum. The tape can also carry additional information; for example, it can be programmed to skip a particular track and repeat another. The music industry delayed releasing prerecorded DAT cassettes because of fears of bootlegging, but a system has now been internationally agreed whereby it is not possible to make more than one copy of any prerecorded compact disc or DAT. DAT is mainly used in recording studios for making master tapes. The system was developed by Sony.

By 1990, DATs for computer data had been developed to a capacity of around 2.5 gigabytes per tape, achieved by using helical scan recording (in which the tape covers some 90% of the total head area of the rotating drum). This enables data from the tape to be read over 200 times faster than it can be written. Any file can be located within 60 seconds.

digital computer computing device that operates on a two-state system, using symbols that are internally coded as binary numbers (numbers made up of combinations of the digits 0 and 1); see ◊computer.

digital data transmission in computing, a way of sending data by converting all signals (whether pictures, sounds, or words) into numeric (normally binary) codes before transmission, then reconverting them on receipt. This virtually eliminates any distortion or degradation of the signal during transmission, storage, or processing.

digital-to-analogue converter electronic circuit that converts a digital signal into an ◊analogue (continuously varying) signal. Such a circuit is used to convert the digital output from a computer into the analogue voltage required to produce sound from a conventional loudspeaker.

digital video interactive powerful compression system used for storing video images on computer; see ◊DVI.

digitizer a device that converts an analogue video signal into a digital format so that video images can be input, stored, displayed, and manipulated by a computer. The term is sometimes used to refer to a ◊graphics tablet.

dingbat non-alphanumeric character, such as a star, bullet, or arrow. Dingbats have been combined into ◊PostScript and ◊TrueType fonts for use with word processors and graphics programs.

DIP abbreviation for *◊document image processing*.

direct access or *random access* type of ◊file access. A direct-access file contains records that can be accessed directly by the computer because each record has its own address on the storage disc.

direct memory access (DMA) a technique used for transferring data to and from external devices without going through the ◊central processing unit and thus speeding up transfer rates. DMA is used for devices such as ◊scanners.

directory a list of file names, together with information that enables a computer to retrieve those files from ◊backing storage. The computer operating system will usually store and update a directory on the backing storage to which it refers. So, for example, on each ◊disc used by a computer a directory file will be created listing the disc's contents.

disc or *disk* in computing, a common medium for storing large volumes

disc
cut-away view of a removable pack of hard discs in a drive unit

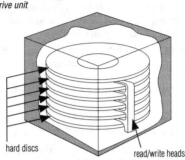

hard discs   read/write heads

of data (an alternative is ◊magnetic tape). A *magnetic disc* is rotated at high speed in a disc-drive unit as a read/write (playback or record) head passes over its surfaces to record or read the magnetic variations that encode the data. Recently, *optical discs*, such as ◊CD-ROM (compact-disc read-only memory) and ◊WORM (write once, read many times), have been used to store computer data. Data are recorded on the disc surface as etched microscopic pits and are read by a laser-scanning device. Optical discs have an enormous capacity – about 550 megabytes (million ◊bytes) on a compact disc, and thousands of megabytes on a full-size optical disc.

Magnetic discs come in several forms: *Fixed hard discs* are built into the disc-drive unit, occasionally stacked on top of one another. A fixed disc cannot be removed: once it is full, data must be deleted in order to free space or a complete new disc drive must be added to the computer system in order to increase storage capacity. Large fixed discs, used with mainframe and minicomputers, provide up to 3,000 megabytes. Small fixed discs for use with microcomputers were introduced in the 1980s and typically hold 40–400 megabytes. *Removable hard discs* are common in minicomputer systems. The discs are contained, individually or as stacks (disc packs), in a protective plastic case, and can be taken out of the drive unit and kept for later use. By swapping such discs around, a single hard-disc drive can be made to provide a potentially infinite storage capacity. However, access speeds and capacities tend to be lower that those associated with large fixed hard discs. A *floppy disc* (or diskette) is the most common form of backing store for microcomputers. It is much smaller in size and capacity than a hard disc, normally holding 0.5–2 megabytes of data. The floppy disc is so called because it is manufactured from thin flexible plastic coated with a magnetic material. The earliest form of floppy disc was packaged in a card case and was easily damaged; more recent versions are contained in a smaller, rigid plastic case and are much more robust. All floppy discs can be removed from the drive unit.

disc compression technique, based on ◊data compression, that makes hard discs and floppy discs appear to have more storage capacity than is normally available. If the data stored on a disc can be compressed to occupy half the original amount of disc space, it will appear that the disc is twice its original size. The processes of compression (to store data) and decompression (so that data can be used) are hidden from the user by the software.

Several commercial disc compression products are available, for example DoubleSpace in ◊MS-DOS 6.0 and Stacker.

disc drive mechanical device that reads data from and writes data to a magnetic ◊disc.

disc drive
floppy disc being inserted into disc drive

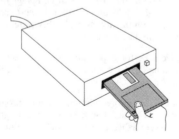

disc formatting preparing a blank magnetic disc so that data can be stored on it. Data are recorded on a disc's surface on circular tracks, each of which is divided into a number of sectors. In formatting a disc, the computer's operating system adds control information such as track and sector numbers, which enables the data stored to be accessed correctly by the disc-drive unit.

disc formatting
surface of a magnetic disc

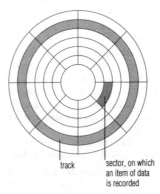

track   sector, on which
an item of data
is recorded

Some floppy discs, called *hard-sectored discs*, are sold already formatted. However, because different makes of computer use different disc formats, discs are also sold unformatted, or *soft-sectored*, and computers are provided with the necessary ◊utility program to format these discs correctly before they are used.

Discman Sony trademark for a portable compact-disc player; the equivalent of a ◊Walkman, it also comes in a model with a liquid-crystal display for data discs.

disc optimizer another name for a ◊defragmentation program, a program that gathers together files that have become fragmented for storage on different areas of a disc. See also ◊fragmentation.

distributed processing computer processing that uses more than one computer to run an application. ◊Local area networks, ◊client–server architecture, and ◊parallel processing involve distributed processing.

dithering in computer graphics, a technique for varying the patterns of dots in an image in order to give the impression of shades of grey. Each dot, however, is of the same size and the same intensity, unlike grey scaling (where each dot can have a different shade) and photographically reproduced half-tones (where the dot size varies).

DLL the abbreviation for ◊*dynamic link library*.

document data associated with a particular application. For example, a *text document* might be produced by a ◊word processor and a *graphics document* might be produced with a ◊CAD package. An ◊*OMR* or ◊*OCR* document is a paper document containing data that can be directly input to the computer using a ◊document reader.

documentation the written information associated with a computer program or ◊applications package. Documentation is usually divided into two categories: program documentation and user documentation.
  Program documentation is the complete technical description of a program, drawn up as the software is written and intended to support any later maintenance or development of that program. It typically includes details of when, where, and by whom the software was written; a general description of the purpose of the software, including recommended input, output, and storage methods; a detailed description of the way the software functions, including full program listings and ◊flow charts; and details of software testing, including sets of ◊test data with expected results. *User documentation* explains how to operate the software. It typically includes a nontechnical explanation of the purpose of the software; instructions for loading, running, and using the software; instructions for preparing any necessary input data; instructions for requesting and interpreting output data; and explanations of any error messages that the program may produce.

document image processing (DIP) scanning documents for storage on ◊CD-ROM. The scanned images are indexed electronically, which provides much faster access than is possible with either paper or ◊microform. See also ◊optical character recognition.

document reader an input device that reads marks or characters, usually on preprepared forms and documents. Such devices are used to capture data by ◊optical mark recognition (OMR), ◊optical character recognition (OCR), and ◊mark sensing.

dongle a device that ensures the legal use of an application program. It is usually attached to the printer port of the computer (between the port and the printer cable) and the program will not run in its absence.

DOS (acronym for *disc operating system*) computer ◊operating system specifically designed for use with disc storage; also used as an alternative name for a particular operating system, ◊MS-DOS.

dot matrix printer computer printer that produces each character individually by printing a pattern, or matrix, of very small dots. The printing head consists of a vertical line or block of either 9 or 24 printing pins. As the printing head is moved from side to side across the paper, the pins are pushed forwards selectively to strike an inked ribbon and build up the dot pattern for each character on the paper beneath.

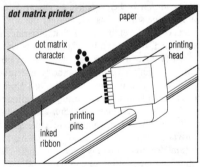

A dot matrix printer is more flexible than a ◊daisywheel printer because it can print graphics and text in many different typefaces. It is cheaper to buy and maintain than a ◊laser printer or ◊ink-jet printer, and, because its pins physically strike the paper, is capable of producing carbon copies. However, it is noisy in operation and cannot produce the high-quality printing associated with the nonimpact printers.

double click to click (press and release a ◊mouse button) twice in quick succession. Double clicking on an ◊icon shown on a ◊graphical user interface (GUI) is used to start an application. In most GUIs it is possible to set the maximum time interval between the two clicks.

double precision a type of ◊floating-point notation that has higher precision, that is, more significant decimal places. The term 'double' is not strictly correct, deriving from such numbers using twice as many ◊bits as standard floating-point notation.

download to retrieve a file from a ◊bulletin board using a ◊modem, or from another computer via a ◊network.

dpi (abbreviation for *dots per inch*) measure of the ◊resolution of images produced by computer screens and printers.

DRAM (acronym for *dynamic random-access memory*) computer memory device in the form of a silicon chip commonly used to provide the ◊immediate access memory of microcomputers. DRAM loses its contents unless they are read and rewritten every 2 milliseconds or so. This process is called *refreshing* the memory. DRAM is slower but cheaper than ◊SRAM, an alternative form of silicon-chip memory.

driver a program that controls a peripheral device. Every device connected to the computer needs a driver program.

The driver ensures that communication between the computer and the device is successful.

For example, it is often possible to connect many different types of printer, each with its own special operating codes, to the same type of computer. This is because driver programs are supplied to translate the computer's standard printing commands into the special commands needed for each printer.

dry running checking by hand (for example, with paper and pencil) the progress of ◊test data through a computer program, before that program is run on a computer.

DTP abbreviation for ◊*desktop publishing*.

dumb terminal a terminal that has no processing capacity of its own but works purely as a means of access to a main ◊central processing unit. Compare with a ◊personal computer used as an intelligent terminal – for example in ◊client–server architecture.

dump the process of rapidly transferring data to external memory or to a printer. It is usually done to help with debugging (see ◊bug) or as part of an error-recovery procedure designed to provide ◊data security. A ◊screen dump makes a printed copy of the current screen display.

DVI (abbreviation for *digital video interactive*) a powerful compression and decompression system for digital video and audio. DVI enables 72 minutes of full-screen, full-motion video and its audio track to be stored on a CD-ROM. Originally developed by the US firm RCA, DVI is now owned by Intel and has active support from IBM and Microsoft. It can be used on the hard disc of a PC as well as on a CD-ROM.

Dvorak keyboard alternative keyboard layout to the normal typewriter keyboard layout (◊QWERTY). In the Dvorak layout the most commonly used keys are situated in the centre, so that keying is faster.

DX suffix used to denote certain chips in ◊Intel's 80x86 range of ◊microprocessors. It was first used 1988 when Intel introduced the 80386SX, a version of the 80386 that was functionally identical to the original, but which communicated more slowly with the rest of the computer. The 80386 was renamed the 80386DX to distinguish it from the SX version. When Intel introduced the 80486DX and 80486SX microprocessors, the DX denoted the fact that the chip had an in-built mathematics ◊coprocessor, whereas the SX version did not.

Subsequent variants of the 80486DX, the 80486DX-2 and 80486DX-4, function faster internally than the 80486DX, but communicate with the rest of the computer at the same speed as the original chip.

dynamic data exchange (DDE) a form of interprocess communication used in Microsoft ◊Windows, providing exchange of commands and data between two applications. DDE is used principally to include live data from one application in another – for example, spreadsheet data in a word-processed report. In Windows 3.1 DDE is enhanced by ◊object linking and embedding.

DDE links between files rely on the files remaining in the same locations in the computer's directory.

dynamic link library (DLL) files of executable functions that can be loaded on demand in Microsoft ◊Windows and linked at run time. Windows itself uses DLL files for handling international keyboards, for example, and Windows word-processing programs use DLL files for functions such as spelling and hyphenation checks, and thesaurus.

E

EBCDIC (abbreviation for *extended binary-coded decimal interchange code*) a code used for storing and communicating alphabetic and numeric characters. It is an 8-bit code, capable of holding 256 different characters, although only 85 of these are defined in the standard version. It is still used in many mainframe computers, but almost all mini- and microcomputers now use ◊ASCII code.

Eckert John Presper Jr 1919– . US electronics engineer and mathematician who collaborated with John Mauchly on the development of the early ENIAC (1946) and UNIVAC 1 (1951) computers.

Eckert was born in Philadelphia, Pennsylvania, and studied at the University of Pennsylvania. During World War II he worked on radar ranging systems and then turned to the design of calculating devices, building the Electronic Numerical Integrator and Calculator (ENIAC) with Mauchly. The Eckert–Mauchly Computer Corporation, formed 1947, was incorporated in Remington Rand 1950 and subsequently came under the control of the Sperry Rand Corporation.

The ENIAC weighed many tonnes and lacked a memory, but could store a limited amount of information and perform mathematical functions. It was used for calculating ballistic firing tables and for meteorological and research problems.

ENIAC was superseded by BINAC, also designed in part by Eckert, and in the early 1950s, Eckert's group began to produce computers for the commercial market with the construction of the UNIVAC 1. Its chief advance was the capacity to store programs.

edge connector an electrical connection formed by taking some of the metallic tracks on a ◊printed circuit board to the edge of the board and using them to plug directly into a matching socket.

Edge connectors are often used to connect the computer's main circuit board, or motherboard, to the expansion boards that provide the computer with extra memory or other facilities.

Because the tracks making the connection would be very difficult to repair if they were to become worn or damaged, edge connectors should not be used to join components that are regularly connected and disconnected.

EDI (abbreviation for *electronic dissemination of information* or *electronic data interchange*) the transfer of structured information in electronic form between computer systems in different organizations. EDI is principally used for exchange of information relating to business transactions and for electronic transfer of funds.

EDP abbreviation for *electronic ◊data processing*.

edutainment (contraction of *education* and *entertainment*) ◊multimedia-related term, used to describe software that is both educational and entertaining. Examples include educational software for children that teaches them to spell or count while playing games, or a ◊CD-ROM about machines that contains animations showing how the machines work. Compare ◊infotainment.

EEPROM (acronym for *electrically erasable programmable read-only memory*) computer memory that can record data and retain it indefinitely. The data can be erased with an electrical charge and new data recorded.

Some EEPROM must be removed from the computer and erased and reprogrammed using a special device. Other EEPROM, called *flash memory*, can be erased and reprogrammed without removal from the computer.

EGA (abbreviation for *enhanced graphics array*) computer colour display system that is better than ◊CGA (colour graphics adapter), providing 16 colours on screen and a resolution of 640×350, but not as good as ◊VGA.

EIS (abbreviation for *executive information systems*) software applications that extract information from an organization's computer applications and data files and present the data in a form required by management.

electronic mail or *e-mail* telecommunications system that enables the users of a computer network to send messages to other users. Telephone wires are used to send the signals from terminal to terminal.

Subscribers to an electronic mail system type messages in ordinary letter form on a word processor, or microcomputer, and 'drop' the letters into a central computer's memory bank by means of a computer/telephone connector (a ◊modem). The recipient 'collects' the letter by calling up the central computer and feeding a unique password into the system.

electronic mail

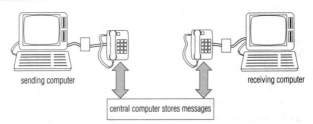

sending computer   receiving computer

central computer stores messages

electronic publishing the distribution of information using computer-based media such as ◊multimedia and ◊hypertext in the creation of electronic 'books'.

Critical technologies in the development of electronic publishing were ◊CD-ROM, with its massive yet compact storage capabilities, and the advent of computer networking with its ability to deliver information instantaneously anywhere in the world.

e-mail abbreviation for ◊*electronic mail*.

emoticon (acronym for *emotion* and *icon*) symbol composed of punctuation marks designed to express some form of emotion in the form of a human face. Emoticons were invented by ◊electronic mail users to overcome the fact that communication using text only cannot convey nonverbal information (body language or vocal intonation) used in ordinary speech.

The following examples should be viewed by turning the page sideways:

:-) smiling   :-O shouting   :-(glum   8-) drunk

EMS abbreviation for ◊*expanded memory specification*.

emulator an item of software or firmware that allows one device to imitate the functioning of another. Emulator software is commonly used to allow one make of computer to run programs written for a different make of computer. This allows a user to select from a wider range of ◊applications programs, and perhaps to save money by running programs designed for an expensive computer on a cheaper model.

Many printers contain emulator firmware that enables them to imitate Hewlett Packard and Epson printers, because so much software is written to work with these widely used machines.

encapsulated PostScript (EPS) computer graphics file format used by the ◊PostScript page-description language. It is essentially a PostScript file with a special structure designed for use by other applications.

encryption providing ◊data security by encoding data so that it is meaningless to unauthorized users who do not have the necessary decoding software.

end user the user of a computer program; in particular, someone who uses a program to perform a task (such as accounting or playing a computer game), rather than someone who writes programs (a programmer).

EPROM (acronym for *erasable programmable read-only memory*) computer memory device in the form of an ◊integrated circuit (chip) that can record data and retain it indefinitely. The data can be erased by exposure to ultraviolet light, and new data recorded. Other kinds of computer memory chips are ◊ROM (read-only memory), ◊PROM (programmable read-only memory), and ◊RAM (random-access memory).

EPS abbreviation for ◊*encapsulated PostScript*.

erasable optical disc another name for a ◊*floptical disc*.

error a fault or mistake, either in the software or on the part of the user, that causes a program to stop running (crash) or produce unexpected results. Program errors, or bugs, are largely eliminated in the course of the programmer's initial testing procedure, but some will remain in most programs. All computer operating systems are designed to produce an *error message* (on the display screen, or in an error file or printout) whenever an error is detected, reporting that an error has taken place and, wherever possible, diagnosing its cause.

error detection the techniques that enable a program to detect incorrect data. A common method is to add a check digit to important codes, such as account numbers and product codes. The digit is chosen so that the code conforms to a rule that the program can verify. Another technique involves calculating the sum (called the ◊hash total) of each instance of a particular item of data, and storing it at the end of the data.

error message message produced by a computer to inform the user that an error has occurred.

Ethernet a protocol for ◊local area networks. Ethernet was developed principally by the Xerox Corporation, but can now be used on many computers. It allows data transfer at rates up to 10 Mbps.

Excel ◊spreadsheet program produced by ◊Microsoft 1985. Versions are available for ◊Windows on the IBM PC and for the Apple Macintosh. Excel pioneered many advanced features in the ease of use of spreadsheets, and has displaced ◊Lotus 1–2–3 as the standard spreadsheet program.

executable file a file – always a program of some kind – that can be run by the computer directly. The file will have been generated from a ◊source program by an ◊assembler or ◊compiler. It will therefore not be coded in ◊ASCII and will not be readable as text. On ◊MS-DOS systems executable files have a .EXE or .COM extension.

execution error or *run-time error* ◊error caused by combinations of data that the programmer did not anticipate.

expanded memory additional memory in an ◊MS-DOS-based computer, usually installed on an expanded-memory board. Expanded memory requires an expanded-memory manager, which gives access to a limited amount of memory at any one time, and is slower to use than ◊extended memory. Software is available under both MS-DOS and ◊Windows to simulate expanded memory for those applications that require it.

expansion board or *expansion card* printed circuit board that can be inserted into a computer in order to enhance its capabilities (for example, to increase its memory) or to add facilities (such as graphics).

expert system computer program for giving advice (such as diagnosing an illness or interpreting the law) that incorporates knowledge derived from human expertise. It is a kind of ◊knowledge-based system containing rules that can be applied to find the solution to a problem. It is a form of ◊artificial intelligence.

export file a file stored by the computer in a standard format so that it can be accessed by other programs, possibly running on different makes of computer.

For example, a word-processing program running on an Apple ◊Macintosh computer may have a facility to save a file on a floppy disc in a format that can be read by a word-processing program running on an IBM PC-compatible computer. When the file is being read by the second program or computer, it is often referred to as an *import file*.

extended memory memory in an ◊MS-DOS-based system that exceeds the 1 Mbyte that DOS supports. Extended memory is not accessible to the ◊operating system and requires an extended memory manager. ◊Windows and Windows applications require extended memory.

F

FAT abbreviation for ◊*file allocation table*.

fax (common name for *facsimile transmission* or *telefax*) the transmission of images over a ◊telecommunications link, usually the telephone network. When placed on a fax machine, the original image is scanned by a transmitting device and converted into coded signals, which travel via the telephone lines to the receiving fax machine, where an image is created that is a copy of the original. Photographs as well as printed text and drawings can be sent. The standard transmission takes place at 4,800 or 9,600 bits of information per second.

fax modem ◊modem capable of transmitting and receiving data in the form of a fax.

A normal fax machine sends data in binary form down a telephone line, in a similar way to a modem. A modem can therefore act as a fax machine, given suitable software. This means a document does not need to be printed before faxing and an incoming fax can be viewed before printing out on a plain-paper printer. However, the computer must be permanently turned on in order to receive faxes.

A separate ◊scanner is needed to fax information created outside the computer (such as a picture).

FDDI (abbreviation for *fibre-optic digital* device interface) a series of network protocols, developed by ◊American National Standards Institute, concerned with high-speed networks using ◊fibre optics cable.

FDDI supports data transmission rates of up to 100 Mb per second and is being introduced in many sites as a replacement for ◊Ethernet. FDDI not only makes possible transmission of large amounts of data, for example colour pictures, but also allows the transmission of voice and video data. See also ◊optical fibres.

feasibility study an initial study undertaken by a systems analyst investigating ways of implementing a new computer system. The likely costs and benefits of the system are estimated, and used to form the basis for deciding whether or not to proceed with the implementation of the system.

feedback general principle whereby the results produced in an ongoing reaction become factors in modifying or changing the reaction; it is the principle used in self-regulating control systems, from a simple thermostat to automatic computer-controlled machine tools. A fully computerized control system, in which there is no operator intervention, is called a *closed-loop feedback* system. A system that also responds to control signals from an operator is called an *open-loop feedback* system.

In self-regulating systems, information about what *is* happening in a system (such as level of temperature, engine speed, or size of workpiece) is fed back to a controlling device, which compares it with what *should* be happening. If the two are different, the device takes suitable action (such as switching on a heater, allowing more steam to the engine, or resetting the tools).

fetch–execute cycle or *processing cycle* the two-phase cycle used by the computer's central processing unit to process the instructions in a program. During the *fetch phase*, the next program instruction is transferred from the computer's immediate access memory to the instruction register (memory location used to hold the instruction while it is being executed). During the *execute phase*, the instruction is decoded and obeyed. The process is repeated in a continuous loop.

fibre optics branch of physics dealing with the transmission of light and images through glass or plastic fibres known as ◊optical fibres.

field a specific item of data. A field is usually part of a *record*, which in turn is part of a ◊file.

field-length check ◊validation check in which the characters in an input field are counted to ensure that the correct number of characters have been entered. For example, a six-figure date field may be checked to ensure that it does contain exactly six digits.

fifth-generation computer anticipated new type of computer based on emerging microelectronic technologies with high computing speeds and ◊parallel processing. The development of very large-scale integration (◊VLSI) technology, which can put many more circuits on to an integrated circuit (chip) than is currently possible, and developments in computer hardware and software design may produce computers far more powerful than those in current use.

file a collection of data or a program stored in a computer's external memory (for example, on ◊disc). It might include anything from information on a company's employees to a program for an adventure game. *Serial files* hold information as a sequence of characters, so that, to read any particular item of data, the program must read all those that precede it. *Random-access files* allow the required data to be reached directly.

file
one form of file structure

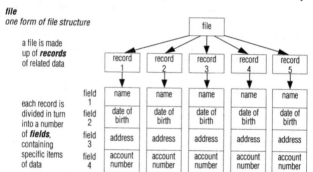

a file is made up of **records** of related data

each record is divided in turn into a number of **fields**, containing specific items of data

Files usually consist of a set of records, each having a number of *fields* for specific items of data. For example, the file for a class of schoolchildren might have a record for each child, with five fields of data in each record, storing: (1) family name; (2) first name; (3) house name or number; (4) street name; (5) town. To find out, for example, which children live in the same street, one would look in field 4.

file access the way in which the records in a file are stored, retrieved, or updated by computer. There are four main types of file organization, each of which allows a different form of access to the records.

Records in a *serial file* are not stored in any particular order, so a specific record can be accessed only by reading through all the previous records.

Records in a *sequential file* are sorted by reference to a key field (see ◊sorting) and the computer can use a searching technique, such as a binary search, to access a specific record.

An *indexed sequential file* possesses an index, which records the position of each block of records and is created and updated with that file. By consulting the index, the computer can obtain the address of the block containing the required record, and search just that block rather than the whole file.

A *direct-access* or *random-access file* contains records that can be accessed directly by the computer.

file allocation table (FAT) a table used by the operating system to record the physical arrangement of files on disc. As a result of ◊fragmentation, files can be split into many parts sited at different places on the disc.

file generation a specific version of a file. When ◊file updating takes place, a new generation of the file is created, containing accurate, up-to-date information. The old generation of the file will often be stored to provide ◊data security in the event that the new generation of the file is lost or damaged.

file librarian or *media librarian* job classification for ◊computer personnel. A file librarian stores and issues the data files used by the computer department.

file merging combining two or more sequentially ordered files into a single sequentially ordered file.

file searching ◊searching a computer memory (usually ◊backing storage) for a file.

file server computer on a ◊network that handles (and usually stores) the data used by other computers on the network. See also ◊client–server architecture.

file sorting arranging files in sequence; see ◊sorting.

file transfer the transmission of a file (data stored on disc, for example) from one machine to another. Both machines must be physically linked (for example, by a telephone line via a ◊modem or ◊acoustic coupler) and both must be running appropriate communications software.

file updating reviewing and altering the records in a file to ensure that the information they contain is accurate and up-to-date. Three basic processes are involved: adding new records, deleting existing records, and amending existing records.

The updating of a ***direct-access file*** is a continuous process because records can be accessed individually and changed at any time. This type of updating is typical of large interactive database systems, such as airline ticket-booking systems. Each time a ticket is booked, files are immediately updated so that double booking is impossible.

file updating
flowchart of the updating of a master file

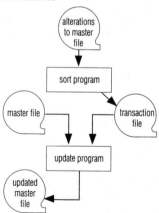

In large commercial applications, however, millions of customer records may be held in a large sequentially ordered file, called the ***master file***. Each time the records in the master file are to be updated (for example, when quarterly bills are being drawn up), a ***transaction file*** must be prepared. This will contain all the additions, deletions, and amendments required to update the master file. The transaction file is sorted into the same order as the master file, then the computer reads both files and produces a new updated ***generation*** of the master file, which will be stored until the next file updating takes place.

filter a program that transforms data. Filters are often used when data output from one application program is input into a different program, which requires a different data format. For example files transferred between two different word-processing programs are run through either an output filter supplied with the first program or an input filter supplied with the second program.

Filters are also used to expand coding structures, which have been simplified for keyboard input, into the often more verbose form required by such standards as SGML (◊Standard Generalized Markup Language).

firmware computer program held permanently in a computer's ◊ROM (read-only memory) chips, as opposed to a program that is read in from external memory as it is needed.

fixed-point notation system in which numbers are represented using a set of digits with the decimal point always in its correct position. For very large and very small numbers this requires a lot of digits. In computing, the size of the numbers that can be handled in this way is limited by the capacity of the computer, and so the slower ◊floating-point notation is often preferred.

flag an indicator that can be set or unset in order to signal whether a particular condition is true – for example, whether the end of a file has been reached, or whether an overflow error has occurred. The indicator usually takes the form of a single binary digit, or bit (either 0 or 1).

flame angry ◊electronic mail message. Users of the ◊Internet use flames to express disapproval of breaches of ◊netiquette. An offensive message posted to, for example, a USENET ◊newsgroup, will cause those offended to flame the culprit. Such flames maintain a level of discipline among the Internet's users.

flash memory type of ◊EEPROM memory that can be erased and reprogrammed without removal from the computer.

flip-flop another name for a ◊bistable circuit.

floating-point notation system in which numbers are represented by means of a decimal fraction and an exponent. For example, in floating-point notation, 123,000,000,000 would be represented as 0.123×10^{12}, where 0.123 is the fraction, or mantissa, and 12 the exponent. The exponent is the power of 10 by which the fraction must be multiplied in order to obtain the true value of the number. floating-point notation enables programs to work with very large and very small numbers using only a few digits; however, it is slower than ◊fixed-point notation and suffers from small rounding errors.

In a computer, numbers expressed in floating-point notation are represented as pairs – for example, 97.8 as (.978, +2) or .978 E2. Decimal numbers are, of course, automatically converted by the computer into binary number code before storage and processing.

floating point unit (FPU) in computing, a specially designed chip that performs floating-point calculations. Computers equipped with an FPU perform certain types of applications much faster than computers that lack one. In particular, graphics applications are faster with an FPU.

Some microprocessors, such as the Intel 80486, have a built-in FPU. With other microprocessors, an FPU can usually be added by inserting the FPU chip on the ◊motherboard.

FLOP (abbreviation for *floating point operations per second*) measure of the speed at which a computer program can be run.

floppy disc a storage device consisting of a light, flexible disc enclosed in a cardboard or plastic jacket. The disc is placed in a disc drive, where it rotates at high speed. Data are recorded magnetically on one or both surfaces.

Floppy discs were invented by IBM in 1971 as a means of loading programs into the computer. They were originally 20 cm/8 in diameter and typically held about 240 ◊kilobytes of data. Present-day floppy

discs, widely used on microcomputers, are usually either 13.3 cm/
5.25 in or 8.8 cm/3.5 in in diameter, and generally hold 0.5–2
◊megabytes, depending on the disc size, recording method, and
whether one or both sides are used.

Floppy discs are inexpensive, and light enough to send through the
post, but have slower access speeds and are more fragile than hard
discs.

floptical disc or *erasable optical disc* a type of optical disc that can
be erased and loaded with new data, just like a magnetic disc. By contrast, most optical discs are read-only. A single optical disc can hold as
much as 1,000 megabytes of data, about 800 times more than a typical
floppy disc. Floptical discs need a special disc drive, but some such drives are also capable of accepting standard 3.5 inch floppy discs.

flow chart diagram, often used to show the possible paths that data
can take through a system or program.

flowchart
program flowchart

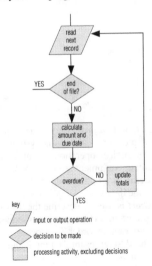

flowchart
system flowchart

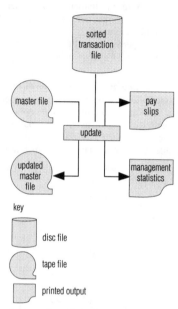

A *system flow chart*, or *data flow chart*, is used to describe the flow of data through a complete data-processing system. Different graphic symbols represent the clerical operations involved and the different input, storage, and output equipment required. Although the flow chart may indicate the specific programs used, no details are given of how the programs process the data.

A *program flow chart* is used to describe the flow of data through a particular computer program, showing the exact sequence of operations performed by that program in order to process the data. Different graphic symbols are used to represent data input and output, decisions, branches, and ◊subroutines.

font or *fount* complete set of printed or display characters of the same typeface, size, and style (bold, italic, underlined, and so on). In the UK, font sizes are measured in points, a point being approximately 0.3 mm.

Fonts used in computer setting are of two main types: bit-mapped and outline. *Bit-mapped fonts* are stored in the computer memory as the exact arrangement of ◊pixels or printed dots required to produce the characters in a particular size on a screen or printer. *Outline fonts* are stored in the computer memory as a set of instructions for drawing the circles, straight lines, and curves that make up the outline of each character. They require a powerful computer because each character is separately generated from a set of instructions and this requires considerable computation. Bit-mapped fonts become very ragged in appearance if they are enlarged and so a separate set of bit maps is required for each font size. In contrast, outline fonts can be scaled to any size and still maintain exactly the same appearance.

font
common fonts

    This is Courier 10 point.
This is Times bold 12 point.
This is Helvetica bold italic 14 point.

footprint the area on the desk or floor required by a computer or other peripheral device.

formatting short for ◊disc formatting.

FORTRAN (acronym for *formula translation*) high-level computer-programming language suited to mathematical and scientific computations. Developed 1956, it is one of the earliest computer languages still in use. A recent version, Fortran 90, is now being used on advanced parallel computers. ◊BASIC was strongly influenced by FORTRAN and is similar in many ways.

fourth-generation language in computing, a type of programming language designed for the rapid programming of ◊applications but often lacking the ability to control the individual parts of the computer. Such a language typically provides easy ways of designing screens and reports, and of using databases. Other 'generations' (the term implies a class of language rather than a chronological sequence) are ◊machine code (first generation); ◊assembly languages, or low-level languages (second); and conventional high-level languages such as ◊BASIC and ◊PASCAL (third).

fractal (from Latin *fractus* 'broken') irregular shape or surface produced by a procedure of repeated subdivision. Generated on a computer screen, fractals are used in computer art, and creating models for geographical or biological processes (for example, the creation of a coastline by erosion or accretion, or the growth of plants).

Fractal compression is a method of storing digitally processed picture images as fractals. It uses less than a quarter of the data produced by breaking down images into ◊pixels. The technique was first used commercially in CD-ROM products 1993.

fragmentation the breaking up of files into many smaller sections stored on different parts of a disc. The computer ◊operating system stores files in this way so that maximum use can be made of disc space. Each section contains a pointer to where the next section is stored. The ◊file allocation table keeps a record of this.

Fragmentation slows down access to files. It is possible to defragment a disc by copying files. In addition, ◊defragmentation programs, or disc optimizers, allow discs to be defragmented without the need for files to be copied to a second storage device.

front-end processor small computer used to coordinate and control the communications between a large mainframe computer and its input and output devices.

ftp (abbreviation for *file transfer protocol*) rules for transferring files between computers on the ◊Internet. The use of ftp avoids incompatibility between individual computers.

Fujitsu Japanese electronics combine, the world's second biggest computer manufacturer (behind IBM) after its purchase of the UK firm ICL in 1990. Fujitsu's turnover in the year ending March 1990 was £9,816 million, of which only 4% was from Europe.

function a small part of a program that supplies a specific value – for example, the square root of a specified number, or the current date. Most programming languages incorporate a number of built-in functions; some allow programmers to write their own. A function may have one or more arguments (the values on which the function operates). A *function key* on a keyboard is one that, when pressed, performs a designated task, such as ending a program.

functional programming computer programming based largely on the definition of ◊functions. There are very few functional programming languages, HOPE and ML being the most widely used, though many more conventional languages (for example, C) make extensive use of functions.

function key key on a keyboard that, when pressed, performs a designated task, such as ending a computer program.

fuzzy logic in mathematics and computing, a form of knowledge representation suitable for notions (such as 'hot' or 'loud') that cannot be defined precisely but depend on their context. For example, a jug of water may be described as too hot or too cold, depending on whether it is to be used to wash one's face or to make tea.

The central idea of fuzzy logic is *probability of set membership*. For instance, referring to someone 175 cm/5 ft 9 in tall, the statement 'this person is tall' (or 'this person is a member of the set of tall people') might be about 70% true if that person is a man, and about 85% true if that person is a woman.

The term 'fuzzy logic' was coined in 1965 by Iranian computer scientist Lofti Zadeh of the University of California at Berkeley, although the core concepts go back to the work of Polish mathematician Jan Lukasiewicz in the 1920s. It has been largely ignored in Europe and the USA, but was taken up by Japanese manufacturers in the mid-1980s and has since been applied to hundreds of electronic goods and industrial machines. For example, a vacuum cleaner launched in 1992 by

Matsushita uses fuzzy logic to adjust its sucking power in response to messages from its sensors about the type of dirt on the floor, its distribution, and its depth. Fuzzy logic enables computerized devices to reason more like humans, responding effectively to complex messages from their control panels and sensors.

G

games console computer capable only of playing games, which are supplied as cartridges that slot directly into the console.

Usually, the price of the console is quite low, while the price of the game cartridges is high.

Games consoles are comparatively low in price with higher quality games than those available on similarly cheap microcomputers. Their disadvantages include the narrow range of software and the incompatibility of one console with another. The best known console manufacturer in the late 1970s was Atari; ◊Nintendo and ◊Sega dominate the market 1994.

gate, logic see ◊logic gate.

Gates Bill (William Henry), III 1955– . US businessman and computer scientist. He is Chief Executive Officer of ◊Microsoft Corporation which he co-founded 1975 with Paul Allen. Gates was responsible for supplying the operating system that ◊IBM chose to use in the IBM PC.

At the time that the deal with IBM was struck, Microsoft did not actually have an operating system, but Gates bought one from another company, renamed it MS-DOS, and modified it to suit IBM's new computer. Microsoft also retained the right to sell MS-DOS to other computer manufacturers, and because the IBM PC was not only successful but easily copied by other manufacturers, MS-DOS found its way onto the vast majority of PCs. The revenue from MS-DOS allowed Microsoft to expand into other areas of software, guided by Gates.

To many people, Gates is Microsoft: most of the company's successes have been his ideas (as have the occasional failures). His life revolves around the company and he expects similar dedication from his staff. In 1994, Gates was successful in fending off both US and

European investigations into anti-competitive practices which could have see Microsoft broken up into smaller companies.

In 1994 he invested $10 million into a biotechnology company, Darwin Molecular, with Paul Allen.

gateway the point of contact between two ◊wide-area networks.

generation stage of development in computer electronics (see ◊computer generation) or a class of programming language (see ◊fourth-generation language).

geographical information system (GIS) computer software that makes possible the visualization and manipulation of spatial data, and links such data with other information such as customer records.

gigabyte a measure of ◊memory capacity, equal to 1,024 ◊megabytes. It is also used, less precisely, to mean 1,000 billion ◊bytes.

GIGO (acronym for *garbage in, garbage out*) expression used to emphasize that inaccurate input data will result in inaccurate output data.

GIS abbreviation for ◊*geographical information system*.

global variable a ◊variable that can be accessed by any program instruction. See also ◊local variable.

Gopher (derived from *go for*) system for searching the ◊Internet for information. Gopher servers use a ◊menu system that allows the user to search the Internet for files based on keywords typed in by the user. In the course of its search it may use the software tools ◊ftp, ◊Archie, ◊Veronica or ◊WAIS without requiring any knowledge of these by the user.

grandfather–father–son system way of providing ◊data security by storing the three most recent versions of a master file, called the *grandfather*, *father*, and *son* generations of the file.

graphical user interface (GUI) or *WIMP* a type of ◊user interface in which programs and files appear as icons (small pictures), user options are selected from pull-down menus, and data are displayed in windows (rectangular areas), which the operator can manipulate in various ways. The operator uses a pointing device, typically a ◊mouse, to make selections and initiate actions.

The concept of the graphical user interface was developed by the Xerox Corporation in the 1970s, was popularized with the Apple Macintosh computers in the 1980s, and is now available on many types of computer – most notably as Windows, an operating system for IBM PC-compatible microcomputers developed by the software company Microsoft.

graphic file format format in which computer graphics are stored and transmitted. There are two main types: ◊raster graphics in which the image is stored as a ◊bit map (arrangement of dots), and ◊vector graphics, in which the image is stored using geometric formulas. There are many different file formats, some of which are used by specific computers, operating systems or applications. Some formats use file compression, particularly those that are able to handle more than one colour. *See table overleaf.*

graphics see ◊computer graphics.

graphics card printed circuit board that, when installed in a computer, permits the computer to display pictures.

graphics tablet or *bit pad* an input device in which a stylus or cursor is moved, by hand, over a flat surface. The computer can keep track of the position of the stylus, so enabling the operator to input drawings or diagrams into the computer.

A graphics tablet is often used with a form overlaid for users to mark boxes in positions that relate to specific registers in the computer, although recent developments in handwriting recognition may increase its future versatility.

common graphic file formats

format	comments
AI	Adobe Illustrator format, subset of EPS
BMP	Windows bit-mapped format
CDR	Coreldraw (graphics program) vector format
CGM	Computer Graphics Metafile; standard vector format
DXF	vector format, created by Autodesk, used by most CAD systems
EPS	Encapsulated PostScript; vector format with TIFF or PICT inclusions
GEM	vector format used by GEM GUI
GIF	bit-mapped format used by CompuServe and other bulletin boards
HPGL	Hewlett-Packard Graphics Language (file extension .plt); vector format
IGES	ANSI standard for three-dimensional (vector) wire models.
PCX, PCC	bit-mapped format, originally devised by ZSoft for PC Paintbrush; now widely used; .pcx is the full-page format and .pcc the cut-out format
PIC	Lotus Picture File; vector format
PICT	Apple Macintosh vector format (file extension .pct)
PIF	IBM vector format
TIFF	bit-mapped format; standard format. Note, however, that there are various flavours of TIFF
WMF	Windows Metafile Format; vector format used for exchanging graphics between Windows applications
WPG	WordPerfect Graphics Format; vector format

graph plotter alternative name for a ◊plotter.

greeking method used in ◊desktop publishing and other page make-up systems for showing type below a certain size on screen. Rather than the actual characters being displayed, either a grey bar or graphics symbols are used. Greeking is usually employed when a general impression of the page lay-out is required.

green computing the gradual movement by computer companies toward incorporating energy-saving measures in the design of systems and hardware. The increasing use of energy-saving devices, so that a computer partially shuts down during periods of inactivity, but can reactivate at the touch of a key, could play a significant role in energy conservation.

It is estimated that worldwide electricity consumption by computers amounts to 240 billion kilowatt hours per year, equivalent to the entire annual consumption of Brazil. In the USA, carbon dioxide emissions could be reduced by 20 million tonnes per year – equivalent to the carbon dioxide output of 5 million cars – if all computers incorporated the latest 'sleep technology' (which shuts down most of the power-consuming features of a computer if it is unused for any length of time).

Although it was initially predicted that computers would mean 'paperless offices', in practice the amount of paper consumed continues to rise. Other environmentally costly features of computers include their rapid obsolescence, health problems associated with monitors and keyboards, and the unfavourable economics of component recycling.

grey scales method of representing continuous tone images on a screen or printer. Each dot in the ⟡bit map is represented by a number of bits and can have a different shade of grey. Compare with ⟡dithering when shades are simulated by altering the density and the pattern of black dots on a white background.

groupware applications software for assisting groups of people working together over a network to coordinate and organize their activity. Such software usually includes ⟡electronic mail facilities and scheduling programs.

GUI abbreviation for ⟡*graphical user interface*.

guiltware variety of ⟡shareware software that attempts to make the user register (and pay for) the software by exploiting the user's sense of guilt. On-screen messages are displayed, usually when the program is started, reminding users that they have an unregistered version of the program that they should pay for if they intend to continue using it. Some programs will also display the message at random intervals while the program is in use.

H

hacking unauthorized access to a computer, either for fun or for malicious or fraudulent purposes. Hackers generally use microcomputers and telephone lines to obtain access. The term is also used in a wider sense to mean using software for enjoyment or self-education, not necessarily involving unauthorized access. See also computer ♢virus.

The 'world's most wanted hacker', Kevin Mitnick, was arrested by US federal agents Feb 1995, accused of stealing thousands of files and credit card numbers.

handshake an exchange of signals between two devices that establishes the communications channels and protocols necessary for the devices to send and receive data.

hard copy computer output printed on paper.

hard disc a storage device usually consisting of a rigid metal ♢disc coated with a magnetic material. Data are read from and written to the disc by means of a disc drive. The hard disc may be permanently fixed into the drive or in the form of a disc pack that can be removed and exchanged with a different pack. Hard discs vary from large units with capacities of more than 3,000 megabytes, intended for use with mainframe computers, to small units with capacities as low as 20 megabytes, intended for use with microcomputers.

hard-sectored disc floppy disc that is sold already formatted, so that ♢disc formatting is not necessary. Usually sectors are marked by holes near the hub of the disc. This system is now obsolete.

hardware the mechanical, electrical, and electronic components of a computer system, as opposed to the various programs, which constitute ♢software.

Hardware associated with a microcomputer might include the power supply and housing of its processor unit, its circuit boards, VDU (screen), disc drive, keyboard, and printer.

hash total a ◊validation check in which an otherwise meaningless control total is calculated by adding together numbers (such as payroll or account numbers) associated with a set of records. The hash total is checked each time data are input, in order to ensure that no entry errors have been made.

HCI abbreviation for ◊*human–computer interaction*.

hertz SI unit (symbol Hz) of frequency (the number of repetitions of a regular occurrence in one second). Radio waves are often measured in megahertz (MHz), millions of hertz, and the ◊clock rate of a computer is usually measured in megahertz. The unit is named after German physicist Heinrich Hertz.

Herzog Bertram 1929– . German-born computer scientist, one of the pioneers in the use of computer graphics in engineering design.

Herzog was born in Offenburg, near Strasbourg, but emigrated to the USA and studied at the Case Institute of Technology. He has alternated academic posts with working in industry. In 1965 he became professor of industrial engineering at the University of Michigan. Two years later he became professor of electrical engineering and computer science at the University of Colorado.

In 1963, Herzog joined the Ford Motor Company as engineering methods manager, where he extensively applied computers to tasks involved in planning and design. Herzog remained as a consultant to Ford after his return to academic life.

heuristics a process by which a program attempts to improve its performance by learning from its own experience.

hexadecimal number system or *hex* number system to the base 16, used in computing. In hex the decimal numbers 0–15 are represented by the characters 0, 1, 2, 3, 4, 5, 6, 7, 8, 9, A, B, C, D, E, F. Hexadecimal numbers are easy to convert to the computer's internal ◊binary number code and are more compact than binary numbers.

Each place in a number increases in value by a power of 16 going from right to left; for instance, 8F is equal to $15 + (8 \times 16) = 143$ in decimal. Hexadecimal numbers are often preferred by programmers writing in low-level languages because they are more easily converted to the computer's internal ◊binary number code than are decimal numbers, and because they are more compact than binary numbers and therefore more easily keyed, checked, and memorized.

hidden file computer file in an ◊MS-DOS system that is not normally displayed when the directory listing command is given. Hidden files include certain system files, principally so that there is less chance of modifying or deleting them by accident, but any file can be made hidden if required.

high-level language a programming language designed to suit the requirements of the programmer; it is independent of the internal machine code of any particular computer. High-level languages are used to solve problems and are often described as *problem-oriented languages* – for example, BASIC was designed to be easily learnt by first-time programmers; COBOL is used to write programs solving business problems; and FORTRAN is used for programs solving scientific and mathematical problems. In contrast, low-level languages, such as ◊assembly languages, closely reflect the machine codes of specific computers, and are therefore described as *machine-oriented languages*.

Unlike low-level languages, high-level languages are relatively easy to learn because the instructions bear a close resemblance to everyday language, and because the programmer does not require a detailed knowledge of the internal workings of the computer. Each instruction in a high-level language is equivalent to several machine-code instructions. High-level programs are therefore more compact than equivalent low-level programs. However, each high-level instruction must be translated into machine code – by either a ◊compiler or an ◊interpreter program – before it can be executed by a computer. High-level languages are designed to be *portable* – programs written in a high-level language can be run on any computer that has a compiler or interpreter for that particular language.

high memory the first 64 kilobytes in the ◊extended memory of an ◊MS-DOS system. The operating system itself is usually installed in this area to allow more conventional memory (below 640 kilobytes) for applications.

hinting a method of reducing the effects of ◊aliasing in the appearance of ◊outline fonts. Hinting makes use of a series of priorities so that noticeable distortions, such as uneven stem weight, are corrected. ◊PostScript Type 1 and ◊TrueType fonts are hinted.

host or *host computer* any computer attached to a ◊network that provides services to other computers. For example, a host may store files used by several other computers or may provide communications facilities to other computers.

The term is also used to mean a computer that is used to develop software to be run on a different type of computer.

hot key a key stroke (or sequence of key strokes) that triggers a memory-resident program. Such programs are called ◊terminate and stay resident. Hot keys should be chosen so that they do not conflict with key sequences in commonly used applications.

HPGL (abbreviation for *Hewlett Packard Graphics Language*) file format used in ◊vector graphics. HPGL is often generated by ◊CAD systems.

HTML (abbreviation for *Hypertext Markup Language*) a ◊Standard Generalized Markup Language (SGML) application used to add codes to ASCII files so that separate files (which can be text, graphics, sound or video) can be linked. This enables programs such as ◊Mosaic to display graphical screens which when ◊clicked upon will jump to another page or ◊download an image, for example, via ◊hyperlinks.

HTML codes also permit ordinary text to be displayed in different fonts and sizes without the need to download the fonts themselves.

human–computer interaction exchange of information between a person and a computer, through the medium of a ◊user interface, studied as a branch of ergonomics.

Hypercard computer application developed for the Apple ◊Macintosh, in which data are stored as if on cards in a card-index system. A group of cards forms a stack. Additional features include the ability to link cards in different ways and, by the use of software buttons (icons that can be clicked or double clicked with a mouse), to access other data. Hypercard is very similar to ◊hypertext, although it does not conform to the rigorous definition of hypertext.

hyperlink link from one document to another or, within the same document, from one place to another. It can be activated by clicking on the link with a ◊mouse. The link is usually highlighted in some way, for example by the inclusion of a small graphic. Documents linked in this way are described as ◊hypertext. Examples of programs that use hypertext and hyperlinks are Windows help files, ◊Acrobat, and ◊Mosaic.

hypertext system for viewing information (both text and pictures) on a computer screen in such a way that related items of information can easily be reached. For example, the program might display a map of a country; if the user clicks (with a ◊mouse) on a particular city, the program will display some information about that city.

I

IBM (abbreviation for *International Business Machines*) multinational company, the largest manufacturer of computers in the world. The company is a descendant of the Tabulating Machine Company, formed 1896 by US inventor Herman Hollerith to exploit his punched-card machines. It adopted its present name 1924. By 1991 it had an annual turnover of $64.8 billion and employed about 345,000 people. In 1992 it made a loss of $4.59 billion.

icon a small picture on the computer screen representing an object or function that the user may manipulate or otherwise use. It is a feature of ◊graphical user interface (GUI) systems. Icons make computers easier to use by allowing the user to point to and click with a ◊mouse on pictures, rather than type commands.

image compression one of a number of methods used to reduce the amount of information required to represent an image, so that it takes up less computer memory and can be transmitted more rapidly and economically via telecommunications systems. It plays a major role in fax transmission and in videophone and multimedia systems.

immediate access memory in computing, ◊memory provided in the ◊central processing unit to store the programs and data in current use.

impact printer computer printer that creates characters by striking an inked ribbon against the paper beneath. Examples of impact printers are dot-matrix printers, daisywheel printers, and most types of line printer.

Impact printers are noisier and slower than nonimpact printers, such as ink-jet and laser printers, but can be used to produce carbon copies.

import file a file that can be read by a program even though it was produced as an ◊export file by a different program or make of computer.

incremental backup a ◊backup copy of only those files that have been modified or created since the last incremental or full backup.

indexed sequential file in computing, a type of ◊file access in which an index is used to obtain the address of the ◊block containing the required record.

information superhighway popular collective name for the ◊Internet and other related large scale computer networks. The term was first used 1993 by US vice president Al Gore in a speech outlining plans to build a high-speed national data communications network.

information technology (IT) collective term for the various technologies involved in processing and transmitting information. They include computing, telecommunications, and microelectronics.

Word processing, databases, and spreadsheets are just some of the computing ◊software packages that have revolutionized work in the office environment. Not only can work be done more quickly than before, but IT has given decisionmakers the opportunity to consider far more data when making decisions.

infotainment (contraction of *information* and *entertainment*) term applied to software that seeks to inform and entertain simultaneously. Many non-fiction ◊CD-ROM titles are classified as infotainment, providing opportunities to learn while playing games or watching animated sequences. Compare ◊edutainment.

ink-jet printer computer printer that creates characters and graphics by spraying very fine jets of quick-drying ink onto paper. Ink-jet printers range in size from small machines designed to work with microcomputers to very large machines designed for high-volume commercial printing.

Because they produce very high-quality printing and are virtually silent, small ink-jet printers (along with ◊laser printers) are replacing impact printers, such as dot-matrix and daisywheel printers, for use with microcomputers.

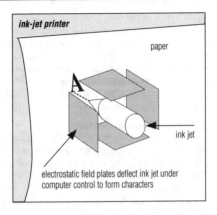

ink-jet printer

paper

ink jet

electrostatic field plates deflect ink jet under computer control to form characters

input device device for entering information into a computer. Input devices include keyboards, joysticks, mice, light pens, touch-sensitive screens, graphics tablets, speech-recognition devices, and vision systems. Compare ◊output device.

Input devices that are used commercially – for example, by banks, postal services, and supermarkets – must be able to read and capture large volumes of data very rapidly. Such devices include document readers for magnetic- ink character recognition (MICR), optical character recognition (OCR), and optical mark recognition (OMR); mark-sense readers; bar-code scanners; magnetic-strip readers; and point-of-sale (POS) terminals. Punched-card and paper-tape readers were used in earlier commercial applications but are now obsolete.

instruction register in computing, a special memory location used to hold the instruction that the computer is currently processing. It is located in the control unit of the ◊central processing unit, and receives instructions individually from the immediate access memory during the fetch phase of the ◊fetch–execute cycle.

instruction set the complete set of machine-code instructions that a computer's ◊central processing unit can obey.

integrated circuit (IC), popularly called *silicon chip*, a miniaturized electronic circuit produced on a single crystal, or chip, of a semiconducting material – usually silicon. It may contain many thousands of components and yet measure only 5 mm/0.2 in square and 1 mm/0.04 in thick. The IC is encapsulated within a plastic or ceramic case, and linked via gold wires to metal pins with which it is connected to a ◊printed circuit board and the other components that make up such electronic devices as computers and calculators.

Integrated Services Digital Network (ISDN) internationally developed telecommunications system for sending signals in ◊digital format along optical fibres and coaxial cable. It involves converting the 'local loop' – the link between the user's telephone (or private automatic branch exchange) and the digital telephone exchange – from an ◊analogue system into a digital system, thereby greatly increasing the amount of information that can be carried. The first large-scale use of ISDN began in Japan 1988.

ISDN has advantages in higher voice quality, better- quality faxes, and the possibility of data transfer between computers faster than current modems. With ISDN's *Basic Rate Access*, a multiplexer divides one voice telephone line into three channels: two B bands and a D band. Each B band offers 64 kilobits per second and can carry one voice conversation or 50 simultaneous data calls at 1,200 bits per second. The D band is a data-signalling channel operating at 16 kilobits per second. With *Primary Rate Access*, ISDN provides 30 B channels.

British Telecom began offering ISDN to businesses 1991, with some 47,000 ISDN-equipped lines. Its adoption in the UK is expected to stimulate the use of data-communications services such as faxing, teleshopping, and home banking. New services may include computer conferencing, where both voice and computer communications take place simultaneously, and videophones.

Intel manufacturer of the ◊microprocessors that form the basis of the IBM PC range and its clones. Recent microprocessors are the 80386 and 80486 (the basis of machines referred to as 386 and 486 PCs), and the ◊Pentium, released in 1993.

Details of the P6 microprocessor were released Feb 1995. It can execute twice as many instructions (17 million per second) in a given time as the Pentium chip it is to replace, as it also analyses software programs to identify the most efficient way of running them.

In 1994 the company held a 90% share of the the global micro-processor market, and, together with Microsoft, supplied operating systems and computer chips for almost 85% of the world's personal computers.

intelligent terminal a ◊terminal with its own processor which can take some of the processing load away from the main computer.

interactive describing a computer system that will respond directly to data or commands entered by the user. For example, most popular pro-grams, such as word processors and spreadsheet applications, are interactive. Multimedia programs are usually highly interactive, allow-ing users to decide what type of information to display (text, graphics, video, or audio) and enabling them (by means of ◊hypertext) to choose an individual route through the information.

interactive computing a system for processing data in which the operator is in direct communication with the computer, receiving imme-diate responses to input data. In ◊batch processing, by contrast, the necessary data and instructions are prepared in advance and processed by the computer with little or no intervention from the operator.

interactive video (IV) computer-mediated system that enables the user to interact with and control information (including text, recorded speech, or moving images) stored on video disc. IV is most commonly used for training purposes, using analogue video discs, but has wider applications with digital video systems such as CD-I (Compact Disc Interactive, from Philips and Sony) which are based on the CD-ROM format derived from audio compact discs.

interface the point of contact between two programs or pieces of equipment. The term is most often used for the physical connection between the computer and a ◊peripheral device, which is used to com-pensate for differences in such operating characteristics as speed, data coding, voltage, and power consumption. For example, a *printer inter-face* is the cabling and circuitry used to transfer data from a computer to a printer, and to compensate for differences in speed and coding.

Common standard interfaces include the *Centronics interface*, used to connect parallel devices, and the *RS232 interface*, used to connect serial devices. For example, in many microcomputer systems, an RS232 interface is used to connect the microcomputer to a modem, and a Centronics device is used to connect it to a printer.

interlacing technique for increasing resolution on computer graphic displays. The electron beam traces alternate lines on each pass, providing twice the number of lines of a non-interlaced screen. However, screen refresh is slower and screen flicker may be increased over that seen on an equivalent non-interlaced screen.

International Organization for Standardization (ISO) international organization founded 1947 to standardize technical terms, specifications, units, and so on. Its headquarters are in Geneva.

Internet global, on-line computer network connecting governments, companies, universities, and many other networks and users. The service offers ◊electronic mail, conferencing and chat services, as well as the ability to access remote computers and send and retrieve files. It began in 1984 and by late 1994 was estimated to have over 40 million users on 11,000 networks in 70 countries, with an estimated one million new users joining each month.

The Internet began with funding from the US National Science Foundation as a means to allow American universities to share the resources of five national supercomputing centres. Its numbers of users quickly grew as access became cheap enough for domestic users to have their own links on personal computers. By the early 1990s the wealth of information made freely available on this network had increased so much that a host of indexing and search services sprang up to answer user demand. Such programmes as Gopher, Veronica, and WAIS (Wide Area Information Service) provide such services through a menu-based interface; the World-Wide Web uses ◊hypertext to allow browsing. *See feature article overleaf.*

interpreter computer program that translates and executes a program written in a high-level language. Unlike a ◊compiler, which produces a complete machine-code translation of the high-level program in one

interpreter
flowchart showing how an interpreter works

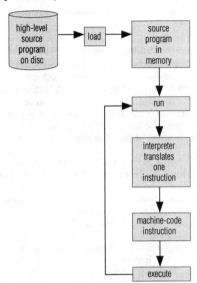

operation, an interpreter translates the source program, instruction by instruction, each time that program is run.

Because each instruction must be translated each time the source program is run, interpreted programs run far more slowly than do compiled programs. However, unlike compiled programs, they can be executed immediately without waiting for an intermediate compilation stage.

interrupt a signal received by the computer's central processing unit that causes a temporary halt in the execution of a program while some other task is performed. Interrupts may be generated by the computer's internal electronic clock (clock interrupt), by an input or output device,

A web of many networks

1994 was the year that a lot of people heard of the Internet for the first time, even though this network that interconnects other networks has been around since the late 1980s and the technology it depends on was pioneered by the US Defense Department's ARPAnet in the 1970s.

ARPAnet was an experiment: the idea was to research building a computer network that could function in the event of partial outages, as if in a bomb attack. The Internet works along the same lines, which involves routing packets of data from one computer to another in any sequence until the data reaches its destination. But unlike the ARPAnet, the Internet grew out of a host of small, independent local area networks owned by companies and other organizations, who could see mutual benefits in being connected to each other. One of the key such networks was NSFnet, named for the USA's National Science Foundation, which needed to ensure that the resources of the five very expensive, regional supercomputing centres it was building could be shared among educational institutions all over the country.

It didn't take long before institutions in other countries began hooking themselves to the Internet, and by 1994 the net was spreading everywhere, totalling some 25 million users worldwide. It's estimated that about 25% of all hosts connected to the Internet are located in Europe. In the USA, development is speeding up since the Clinton administration has announced its intention to build a National Information Infrastructure (NII) that will be the data equivalent of the high-speed Interstate road system. As part of this initiative, the White House itself got connected to the Internet in 1993, and uses the Internet to disseminate official government information and to accept electronic mail to the president and vice-president.

The explosion of interest in the Internet in 1994 was largely fuelled by the advent of affordable Internet access for people outside universities, government organizations, and the big computing companies. Commercial on-line services such as Delphi, America Online, and CompuServe all launched Internet gateways in 1994. Specialist providers of dial-up Internet connections had proved extremely popular in both the USA and the UK over the previous couple of years.

But the point of the Internet isn't to deploy technology around the world; the point is to make it possible to share information instantly. Over a dial-up Internet connection, for example, from a desk in London you can view paintings from the Louvre on a computer in Paris; pick up a copy of USA talk show host David Letterman's latest Top Ten list off a computer in the USA; check out player biographies during the World Cup from a computer in Cambridge (UK); and, more practically, browse a database of more than 15,000 publications in Colorado and order specific articles to be sent by fax. Except for the fax part, all of that is free once your Internet connection is paid for.

A lot of talk goes on as well, both privately by electronic mail (e-mail) and publicly, over USENET. USENET is not actually part of the Internet, although many people confuse the two. USENET is a feed of news, data, and general discussion that is propagated around the world by a number of means, one of which is the Internet. USENET is organized into topics, known as newsgroups. The names generally give a pretty good idea of what the newsgroups are about: alt.fan.letterman, rec.sport.tennis, news.newusers.questions, alt.sex, or uk.misc.

In the first two weeks of July 1994, one site (UUnet) calculated that 845,238 articles (the USENET word for messages of any length) were distributed by this means by 183,773 different users to 10,205 different newsgroups for a total of 1,657Mb. That's an average of 118Mb per day.

The Internet is changing all the time because it has such a large community of technically sophisticated users who write tools they need for their own work and then distribute them. The file you need is almost certainly out there somewhere, but where? In the early 1990s, therefore, various users started building indexing and search tools that let you scan the net. The first of these, Archie, Veronica, Gopher, and WAIS servers, were all text-based. But a lot of the excitement in 1993 and 1994 was over the World-Wide Web. Developed at CERN, the European particle physics laboratory, the World-Wide Web uses hypertext to let you browse the net in an intuitive manner. Tools like this are what will make the Internet usable by everyone.

Wendy Grossman

or by a software routine. After the computer has completed the task to which it was diverted, control returns to the original program.

For example, many computers, while printing a long document, allow the user to carry on with other work. When the printer is ready for more data, it sends an interrupt signal that causes the computer to halt work on the user's program and transmit more data to the printer.

inverse video or *reverse video* a display mode in which images on a display screen are presented as a negative of their normal appearance. For example, if the computer screen normally displays dark images on a light background, inverse video will change all or part of the screen to a light image on a dark background. Inverse video is commonly used to mark out text and pictures that the user wishes the computer to change in some way. For example, the user of a word-processing program might use a ◊mouse to mark in inverse video a paragraph of text that is to be deleted from the document.

inverted file a file that reorganizes the structure of an existing data file to enable a rapid search to be made for all records having one field falling within set limits.

For example, a file used by an estate agent might store records on each house for sale, using a reference number as the key field for ◊sorting. One field in each record would be the asking price of the house. To speed up the process of drawing up lists of houses falling within certain price ranges, an inverted file might be created in which the records are rearranged according to price. Each record would consist of an asking price, followed by the reference numbers of all the houses offered for sale at this approximate price.

I/O (abbreviation for *input/output*) see ◊input devices and ◊output devices. The term is also used to describe transfer to and from disc – that is, disc I/O.

ISA bus (abbreviation for *industry standard architecture bus*) a data ◊bus used by IBM PCs based on ◊Intel 8086 and 80x86 microprocessors.

ISDN abbreviation for ◊*Integrated Services Digital Network*, a telecommunications system.

ISO abbreviation for ⟳*International Organization for Standardization*.

IT abbreviation for ⟳*information technology*.

iteration a method of solving a problem by performing the same steps repeatedly until a certain condition is satisfied. For example, in one method of ⟳sorting, adjacent items are repeatedly exchanged until the data are in the required sequence.

J

Jobs Steve (Steven Paul) 1955–   . US computer scientist. He co-founded ◊Apple Computer Inc with Steve Wozniak 1976, and founded ◊NeXT Technology Inc.

Jobs holds a unique position in the personal computer industry, having been responsible for the creation of three different types of computer. He produced the popular Apple II personal computer, but his greatest success came with the Apple ◊Macintosh 1984, marketed as 'the computer for the rest of us'. A decline in Apple's fortunes led to Jobs' departure and the setting up of NeXT. The NeXT computer met limited commercial success, but its many innovative ideas, particularly in the use of ◊object-oriented programming technology, have found their way into mainstream computing.

joystick an input device that signals to a computer the direction and extent of displacement of a hand-held lever. It is similar to the joystick used to control the flight of an aircraft.

Joysticks are sometimes used to control the movement of a cursor (marker) across a display screen, but are much more frequently used to provide fast and direct input for moving the characters and symbols that feature in computer games. Unlike a ◊mouse, which can move a pointer in any direction, simple games joysticks are often capable only of moving an object in one of eight different directions.

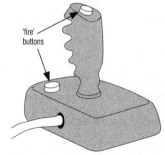

'fire' buttons

JPEG (abbreviation for *Joint Photographic Experts Group*) used to describe a compression standard set up by that group and now widely accepted for the storage and transmission of colour images.

jump a programming instruction that causes the computer to branch to a different part of a program, rather than execute the next instruction in the program sequence. Unconditional jumps are always executed; conditional jumps are only executed if a particular condition is satisfied.

justification in printing and word processing, the arrangement of text so that it is aligned with either the left or right margin, or both.

Left-justified text has lines of different length that are perfectly aligned with the left margin but not with the right margin. The left margin is straight but the right margin is uneven, or ragged. *Right-justified text*, normally only used for columns of numbers, has lines of different length that are perfectly aligned with the right margin but not with the left margin. The right margin is straight but the left margin is ragged. *Fully justified text* has lines of the same length that are perfectly aligned with both the left and the right margins. Both margins are

> This is an example of text that is left justified. The lines are of unequal length and are aligned with the left margin
>
> This is an example of text that is right justified. The lines are of unequal length and are aligned with the right margin
>
> This is an example of text that is fully justified. The lines are of equal length and are aligned with both the left and the right margins.

even. Many word processors can automatically produce fully justified text by inserting extra spaces between the words in each line, or by adjusting the spacing between the letters (microspacing).

K

kermit a widely used file-transfer protocol (◊ftp), originally developed at Columbia University and made available without charge. Kermit is available as part of most communications packages and available on most operating systems.

The UK centre for kermit distribution is at the University of Lancaster.

keyboard an input device resembling a typewriter keyboard, used to enter instructions and data. There are many variations on the layout and labelling of keys. Extra numeric keys may be added, as may special-purpose function keys, whose effects can be defined by programs in the computer.

keyboard
typical computer keyboard

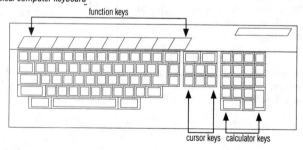

function keys

cursor keys   calculator keys

key field a selected field, or portion, of a record that is used to identify that record uniquely; in a file of records it is the field used as the basis for ◊sorting the file. For example, in a file containing details of a bank's customers, the customer account number would probably be used as the key field.

key-to-disc system or _key-to-tape system_ a system that enables large amounts of data to be entered at a keyboard and transferred directly onto computer-readable discs or tapes.

Such systems are used in ◊batch processing, in which batches of data, prepared in advance, are processed by computer with little or no intervention from the user. The preparation of the data may be controlled by a minicomputer, freeing a larger, mainframe computer for the task of processing.

killer application a program so good or so compelling to certain potential users that they buy the computer that the program runs on for no other reason than to be able to use that program.

Killer applications are very rare. The most successful was VisiCalc, the first spreadsheet to run on a personal computer (the original Apple microcomputer). VisiCalc succeeded as a killer application because it provided a unique tool for accountants to manipulate numbers easily without the need for programming skills.

The only other clear example is PageMaker, the first desktop publishing program, which was responsible for selling the Apple ◊Macintosh to the design and publishing community.

kilobyte (K or KB) a unit of memory equal to 1,024 ◊bytes. It is sometimes used, less precisely, to mean 1,000 bytes.

In the metric system, the prefix 'kilo-' denotes multiplication by 1,000 (as in kilometre, a unit equal to 1,000 metres). However, computer memory size is based on the ◊binary number system, and the most convenient binary equivalent of 1,000 is 2^{10}, or 1,024.

knowledge-based system (KBS) computer program that uses an encoding of human knowledge to help solve problems. It was discovered during research into ◊artificial intelligence that adding heuristics (rules of thumb) enabled programs to tackle problems that were otherwise difficult to solve by the usual techniques of computer science.

Chess-playing programs have been strengthened by including knowledge of what makes a good position, or of overall strategies, rather than relying solely on the computer's ability to calculate variations.

L

LAN abbreviation for ◊*local area network*.

laptop computer portable microcomputer, small enough to be used on the operator's lap. It consists of a single unit, incorporating a keyboard, ◊floppy disc or ◊hard disc drives, and a screen. The screen often forms a lid that folds back in use. It uses a liquid-crystal or gas-plasma display, rather than the bulkier and heavier cathode-ray tubes found in most display terminals. A typical laptop computer measures about 210×297 mm/8.3×11.7 in (A4), is 5 cm/2 in thick, and weighs less than 3 kg/6 lb 9 oz.

laser printer computer printer in which the image to be printed is formed by the action of a laser on a light-sensitive drum, then transferred to paper by means of an electrostatic charge. Laser printers are page printers, printing a complete page at a time. The printed image, which can take the form of text or pictures, is made up of tiny dots, or ink particles. The quality of the image generated depends on the fineness of these dots – most laser printers can print up to 120 dots per cm/300 dots per in across the page.

A typical desktop laser printer can print about 4–20 pages per minute. The first low-cost laser printer suitable for office use appeared in 1984.

Laser printers range in size from small machines designed to work with microcomputers to very large machines designed for high-volume commercial printing. Because they produce very high-quality print and are virtually silent, small laser printers (along with ◊ink-jet printers) have replaced ◊dot matrix printers and ◊daisywheel printers as the most popular type of microcomputer printer.

LCD abbreviation for ◊*liquid-crystal display*.

LED abbreviation for ◊*light-emitting diode*.

library program one of a collection, or library, of regularly used software routines, held in a computer backing store. For example, a programmer might store a routine for sorting a file into ◊key field order, and so could incorporate it easily into any new program being developed instead of having to rewrite it.

light-emitting diode (LED) means of displaying symbols in electronic instruments and devices. An LED is made of semiconductor material, such as gallium arsenide phosphide, that glows when electricity is passed through it. The first digital watches and calculators had LED displays, but many later models use ◊liquid-crystal displays.

In 1993 chemists at the University of Cambridge, England, developed LEDs from the polymer poly(*p*-phenylenevinyl) (PPV) that emit as much light as conventional LEDs and in a variety of colours.

light pen a device resembling an ordinary pen, used to indicate locations on a computer screen. With certain computer-aided design (◊CAD) programs, the light pen can be used to instruct the computer to change the shape, size, position, and colours of sections of a screen image.

The pen has a photoreceptor at its tip that emits signals when light from the screen passes beneath it. From the timing of this signal and a gridlike representation of the screen in the computer memory, a computer program can calculate the position of the light pen.

line printer computer ♦printer that prints a complete line of characters at a time. Line printers can achieve very high printing speeds of up to 2,500 lines a minute, but can print in only one typeface, cannot print graphics, and are very noisy. Until the late 1980s they were the obvious choice for high-volume printing, but high-speed ♦page printers, such as laser printers, are now preferred.

liquid-crystal display (LCD) display of numbers (for example, in a calculator) or pictures (such as on a pocket television screen) produced by molecules of a substance in a semiliquid state with some crystalline properties, so that clusters of molecules align in parallel formations. The display is a blank until the application of an electric field, which 'twists' the molecules so that they reflect or transmit light falling on them.

LISP (contraction of *list processing*) high-level computer-programming language designed for manipulating lists of data items. It is used primarily in research into ♦artificial intelligence (AI).

Developed in the 1960s, and until recently common only in university laboratories, LISP is used more in the USA than in Europe, where the language ♦PROLOG is often preferred for AI work.

local area network (LAN) in computing, a ♦network restricted to a single room or building. Local area networks enable around 500 devices to be connected together.

local bus an extension of the central processing unit (CPU) ♦bus (electrical pathway), designed to speed up data transfer between the CPU, discs, graphics boards, and other devices. There are two common specifications, VESA and ♦PCI, but PCI is likely to become standard in the 1990s.

local variable a ♦variable that can be accessed only by the instructions within a particular ♦subroutine.

logical error an ♦error in the program's design. A logical error may cause a program to fail to respond in the correct way to user requests or to crash completely.

logic gate or *logic circuit* in electronics, one of the basic components used in building ♦integrated circuits. The five basic types of gate make

logic gate
circuit symbols

input input — output | OR gate | AND gate | NOT or inverter gate | NOR gate | NAND gate

truth tables

inputs		output
0	0	0
0	1	1
1	0	1
1	1	1

OR gate

inputs		output
0	0	0
0	1	0
1	0	0
1	1	1

AND gate

inputs	output
0	1
1	0

NOT gate

inputs		output
0	0	1
0	1	0
1	0	0
1	1	0

NOR gate

inputs		output
0	0	1
0	1	1
1	0	1
1	1	0

NAND gate

logical decisions based on the functions NOT, AND, OR, NAND (NOT AND), and NOR (NOT OR). With the exception of the NOT gate, each has two or more inputs.

Information is fed to a gate in the form of binary-coded input signals (logic value 0 stands for 'off' or 'low-voltage pulse', logic 1 for 'on' or 'high-voltage'), and each combination of input signals yields a specific output (logic 0 or 1). An *OR* gate will give a logic 1 output if one or more of its inputs receives a logic 1 signal; however, an *AND* gate will yield a logic 1 output only if it receives a logic 1 signal through both its inputs. The output of a *NOT* or *inverter* gate is the opposite of the signal received through its single input, and a *NOR* or *NAND* gate produces an output signal that is the opposite of the signal that would have been produced by an OR or AND gate respectively. The properties of a logic gate, or of a combination of gates, may be defined and presented in the form of a diagram called a *truth table*, which lists the output that will be triggered by each of the possible combinations of input signals. The process has close parallels in computer programming, where it forms the basis of binary logic.

LOGO (Greek *logos* 'word') high-level computer programming language designed to teach mathematical concepts. Developed about 1970 at the Massachusetts Institute of Technology, it became popular in schools and with home computer users because of its 'turtle graphics' feature. This allows the user to write programs that create line drawings on a computer screen, or drive a small mobile robot (a 'turtle' or 'buggy') around the floor.

LOGO encourages the use of languages in a logical and structured way, leading to 'microworlds', in which problems can be solved by using a few standard solutions.

log off or *log out* the process by which a user identifies himself or herself to a multi-user computer and leaves the system.

log on or *log in* the process by which a user identifies himself or herself to a multiuser computer and enters the system. Logging on usually requires the user to enter a password before access is allowed.

look-and-feel the general appearance of a user interface (usually a ◊graphical user interface). The concept of look-and-feel was the subject of a court case in the USA, when ◊Apple sued ◊Microsoft on the basis that the look-and-feel of Microsoft ◊Windows infringed their copyright. The case was decided principally in Microsoft's favour.

loop short for ◊program loop.

Lotus 1–2–3 ◊spreadsheet computer program, produced by Lotus Development Corporation. It first appeared in 1982 and its combination of spreadsheet, graphics display, and data management contributed to the rapid acceptance of the IBM Personal Computer in businesses.

low-level language a programming language designed for a particular computer and reflecting its internal ◊machine code; low-level languages are therefore often described as *machine-oriented* languages. They cannot easily be converted to run on a computer with a different central processing unit, and they are relatively difficult to learn because a detailed knowledge of the internal working of the computer is required. Since they must be translated into machine code by an ◊assembler program, low-level languages are also called ◊assembly languages.

A mnemonic-based low-level language replaces binary machine-code instructions, which are very hard to remember, write down, or correct, with short codes chosen to remind the programmer of the instructions they represent. For example, the binary-code instruction that means '*st*ore the contents of the *a*ccumulator' may be represented with the mnemonic STA.

In contrast, ◊high-level languages are designed to solve particular problems and are therefore described as ***problem-oriented languages***.

LSI (abbreviation for ***large-scale integration***) the technology that enables whole electrical circuits to be etched into a piece of semiconducting material just a few millimetres square.

By the late 1960s a complete computer processor could be integrated on a single chip, or ◊integrated circuit, and in 1971 the US electronics company Intel produced the first commercially available ◊microprocessor. Very large-scale integration (◊VLSI) results in even smaller chips.

M

machine code a set of instructions that a computer's central processing unit (CPU) can understand and obey directly, without any translation. Each type of CPU has its own machine code. Because machine-code programs consist entirely of binary digits (bits), most programmers write their programs in an easy-to-use ◊high-level language. A high-level program must be translated into machine code – by means of a ◊compiler or ◊interpreter program – before it can be executed by a computer.

Where no suitable high-level language exists or where very efficient machine code is required, programmers may choose to write programs in a low-level, or assembly, language, which is eventually translated into machine code by means of an ◊assembler program.

Microprocessors (CPUs based on a single integrated circuit) may be classified according to the number of machine-code instructions that they are capable of obeying: ◊CISC (complex instruction set computer) microprocessors support up to 200 instructions, whereas ◊RISC (reduced instruction set computer) microprocessors support far fewer instructions but execute programs more rapidly.

machine-readable of data, readable directly by a computer without the need for retyping. The term is usually applied to files on disc or tape, but can also be applied to typed or printed text that can be scanned for ◊optical character recognition.

Macintosh range of microcomputers produced by Apple Computers. The Apple Macintosh, introduced in 1984, was the first popular microcomputer with a ◊graphical user interface.

The success of the Macintosh prompted other manufacturers and software companies to create their own graphical user interfaces. Most notable of these are Microsoft Windows, which runs on IBM PC-compatible microcomputers, and OSF/Motif, from the Open Software Foundation, which is used with many Unix systems. In 1994 Apple licensed the Macintosh for the first time, thus enabling other manufacturers to make cheaper machines.

macro in computer programming, a new command created by combining a number of existing ones. For example, if a programming language has separate commands for obtaining data from the keyboard and for displaying data on the screen, the programmer might create a macro that performs both these tasks with one command. A *macro key* on the keyboard combines the effects of pressing several individual keys.

magnetic-ink character recognition (MICR) a technique that enables special characters printed in magnetic ink to be read and input rapidly to a computer. MICR is used extensively in banking because magnetic-ink characters are difficult to forge and are therefore ideal for marking and identifying cheques.

magnetic-ink character recognition

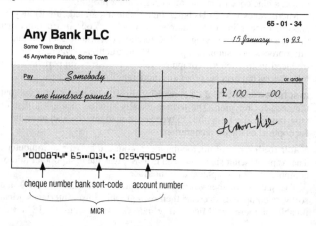

magnetic strip or *magnetic stripe* thin strip of magnetic material attached to a plastic card (such as a credit card) and used for recording data.

magnetic tape narrow plastic ribbon coated with an easily magnetizable material on which data can be recorded. For mass storage on commercial mainframe computers, large reel-to-reel tapes are still used, but cartridges are coming in. Various types of cartridge are now standard on minis and PCs, while audio cassettes are sometimes used with home computers.

mail merge a feature offered by some word-processing packages that enables a list of personal details, such as names and addresses, to be combined with a general document outline to produce individualized documents.

For example, a club secretary might create a file containing a mailing list of the names and addresses of the club members. Whenever a letter is to be sent to all club members, a general letter outline is prepared with indications as to where individual names and addresses need to be added. The mail-merge feature then combines the file of names and addresses with the letter outline to produce and print individual letters addressed to each club member.

mainframe large computer used for commercial data processing and other large-scale operations. Because of the general increase in computing power, the differences between the mainframe, ◊supercomputer, ◊minicomputer, and ◊microcomputer (personal computer) are becoming less marked.

Mainframe manufacturers include IBM, Amdahl, Fujitsu, and Hitachi. Typical mainframes have from 32 to 256 Mb of memory and tens of gigabytes of disc storage.

mark sensing a technique that enables pencil marks made in predetermined positions on specially prepared forms to be rapidly read and input to a computer. The technique makes use of the fact that pencil marks contain graphite and therefore conduct electricity. A *mark sense reader* scans the form by passing small metal brushes over the paper surface. Whenever a brush touches a pencil mark a circuit is completed and the mark is detected.

mass storage system a backing-store system, such as a library of magnetic-tape cartridges, capable of storing very large amounts of data.

master file a file that is the main source of data for a particular application. Various methods of ◊file updating are used to ensure that the data in the master file is accurate and up to date.

media (singular *medium*) the collective name for materials on which data can be recorded. For example, paper is a medium that can be used to record printed data; a floppy disc is a medium for recording magnetic data.

media librarian alternative name for a ◊*file librarian.*

megabyte (Mb) a unit of memory equal to 1,024 ◊kilobytes.
    It is sometimes used, less precisely, to mean 1 million bytes.

memory the part of a system used to store data and programs either permanently or temporarily. There are two main types: immediate access memory and backing storage. Memory capacity is measured in ◊bytes or, more conveniently, in kilobytes (units of 1,024 bytes) or megabytes (units of 1,024 kilobytes).
    Immediate access memory, or *internal memory*, describes the memory locations that can be addressed directly and individually by the central processing unit. It is either read-only (stored in ROM, PROM, and EPROM chips) or read/write (stored in RAM chips). Read-only memory stores information that must be constantly available and is unlikely to be changed. It is nonvolatile – that is, it is not lost when the computer is switched off. Read/write memory is volatile – it stores programs and data only while the computer is switched on.
    Backing storage, or *external memory*, is nonvolatile memory, located outside the central processing unit, used to store programs and data that are not in current use. Backing storage is provided by such devices as magnetic ◊discs (floppy and hard discs), ◊magnetic tape (tape streamers and cassettes), optical discs (such as ◊CD-ROM), and ◊bubble memory. By rapidly switching blocks of information between the backing storage and the immediate access memory, the limited size of the immediate access memory may be increased artificially. When this technique is used to give the appearance of a larger internal memory than physically exists, the additional capacity is referred to as ◊virtual memory.

memory resident present in the main (◊RAM) memory of the computer. For an application to be run, it has to be memory resident. Some applications are kept in memory (see ◊terminate and stay resident), while most are deleted from the memory when their task is complete. However, the memory is usually not large enough to hold all applications and ◊swapping in and out of memory is necessary. This slows down the application.

menu a list of options, displayed on screen, from which the user may make a choice – for example, the choice of services offered to the customer by a bank cash dispenser: withdrawal, deposit, balance, or statement. Menus are used extensively in ◊graphical user interface (GUI) systems, where the menu options are often selected using a pointing device called a ◊mouse.

MICR abbreviation for ◊*magnetic-ink character recognition*.

microchip popular name for the silicon chip, or ◊integrated circuit.

microcomputer or *micro* or *personal computer* small desktop or portable computer, typically designed to be used by one person at a time, although individual computers can be linked in a network so that users can share data and programs.

Its central processing unit is a ◊microprocessor, contained on a single integrated circuit.

Microcomputers are the smallest of the four classes of computer (the others are ◊supercomputer, ◊mainframe, and ◊minicomputer). Since the appearance in 1975 of the first commercially available microcomputer, the Altair 8800, micros have become widely accepted in commerce, industry, and education.

microfiche sheet of film on which printed text is photographically reduced.

microform generic name for media on which text or images are photographically reduced. The main examples are *microfilm* (similar to the film in an ordinary camera) and *microfiche* (flat sheets of film, generally 105 mm/4 in × 148 mm/6 in, holding the equivalent of 420 standard pages). Microform has the advantage of low reproduction and storage costs, but it requires special devices for reading the text. It is widely used for archiving and for storing large volumes of text, such as library catalogues.

Computer data may be output directly and quickly in microform by means of COM (computer output on microfilm/microfiche) techniques.

microprocessor complete computer ◊central processing unit contained on a single ◊integrated circuit, or chip. The appearance of the first microprocessor 1971 designed by Intel for a pocket calculator manufacturer heralded the introduction of the microcomputer. The microprocessor has led to a dramatic fall in the size and cost of computers, and ◊dedicated computers can now be found in washing machines, cars, and so on. Examples of microprocessors are the Intel 8086 family and the Motorola 68000 family.

Microsoft US software corporation, now the world's largest supplier. Microsoft's first major product was ◊MS-DOS, written for IBM, but it has increased its hold on the personal computer market with the release of ◊Windows and related applications.

Together with ◊Intel, the company supplied operating systems and computer chips for almost 85% of the world's personal computers 1994, while 70% carried Microsoft's own MS-DOS operating system. This virtual monopoly was challenged Nov 1994, when its main competitors, IBM, Apple, and Motorola, announced a joint venture to develop a universal PC model.

A US federal probe into charges that Microsoft was engaging in anticompetitive behaviour was carried out 1990–93, from which date the US Justice Department launched its own investigations.

MIDI (acronym for *musical instrument digital interface*) manufacturer's standard allowing different pieces of digital music equipment used in composing and recording to be freely connected.

The information-sending device (any electronic instrument) is called a controller, and the reading device (such as a computer) the sequencer. Pitch, dynamics, decay rate, and stereo position can all be transmitted via the interface. A computer with a MIDI interface can input and store the sounds produced by the connected instruments, and can then manipulate these sounds in many different ways. For example, a single keystroke may change the key of an entire composition. Even a full written score for the composition may be automatically produced.

minicomputer multiuser computer with a size and processing power between those of a ◊mainframe and a ◊microcomputer. Nowadays almost all minicomputers are based on ◊microprocessors.

Minicomputers are often used in medium-sized businesses and in university departments handling ◊database or other commercial programs and running scientific or graphical applications.

mips (acronym for *million instructions per second*) a measure of the speed of a processor. It does not equal the computer power in all cases.

The original IBM PC had a speed of one-quarter mips, but now 50 mips PCs and 100 mips workstations are available.

mnemonic a short sequence of letters used in low-level programming languages (see ◊low-level language) to represent a ◊machine code instruction.

modem (acronym for *modulator/demodulator*) device for transmitting computer data over telephone lines. Such a device is necessary because the ◊digital signals produced by computers cannot, at present, be transmitted directly over the telephone network, which uses ◊analogue signals. The modem converts the digital signals to analogue, and back again. Modems are used for linking remote terminals to central computers and enable computers to communicate with each other anywhere in the world.

monitor alternative term for a ◊*screen.*

morphing the metamorphosis of one shape or object into another by computer-generated animation. First used in filmmaking 1990, it has transformed cinema special effects. Conventional animation is limited to two dimensions; morphing enables the creation of three-dimensional transformations.

To create such effects, the start and end of the transformation must be specified on screen using a wire-frame model that mathematically defines the object. To make the object three-dimensional, the wire can be extruded from a cross-section or turned as on a lathe to produce an evenly turned surface. This is then rendered, or filled in and shaded. Once the beginning and end objects have been created the computer can calculate the morphing process.

Morphing is a lengthy process as every detail about the object's colour, lighting, reflectiveness, surface texture, transparency, and location must be specified. A technique known as 'ray tracing' calculates how the light directed at the object reaches it, with what intensity, and in what areas. The computer then calculates the colour intensity of each pixel (single dot on the screen) that makes up the object.

Morphing has many scientific uses; for example, it can be used by a palaeontologist to reconstruct a skull from a handful of teeth.

Mosaic program that allows the user to search for and view data. Mosaic provides a graphical interface to the ◊Internet via the ◊World-Wide Web and ◊HTML. It was developed by the National Center for Supercomputing Applications at the University of Illinois and is available as freeware. Versions are available for the IBM PC, Apple Macintosh and Unix (under ◊X-Windows).

Most commercial suppliers of Internet services distribute Mosaic to their customers because of the way that it allows even novices to navigate the Internet.

motherboard ◊printed circuit board that contains the main components of a microcomputer. The power, memory capacity, and capability of the microcomputer may be enhanced by adding expansion boards to the motherboard.

Motorola US semiconductor and electronics company. Motorola is best known for the 68000 series of microprocessors used by the Apple ◊Macintosh range and other computers. It also manufactures the ◊PowerPC.

mouse an input device used to control a pointer on a computer screen. It is a feature of ◊graphical user interface (GUI) systems. The mouse is about the size of a pack of playing cards, is connected to the computer by a wire, and incorporates one or more buttons that can be pressed. Moving the mouse across a flat surface causes a corresponding movement of the pointer. In this way, the operator can manipulate objects on the screen and make menu selections.

mouse

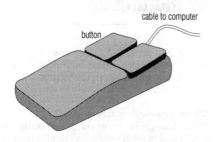

MPC (abbreviation for *Multimedia PC*) standard defining the minimum specification for developing and running CD-ROM software.

MS-DOS (abbreviation for *Microsoft Disc Operating System*) computer ◊operating system produced by Microsoft Corporation, widely used on ◊microcomputers with Intel × 86 family microprocessors. A version called PC-DOS is sold by IBM specifically for its personal computers. MS-DOS and PC-DOS are usually referred to as DOS. MS-DOS first appeared 1981, and was similar to an earlier system from Digital Research called CP/M.

MTBF (abbreviation for *mean time between failures*) the statistically average time a component can be used before it goes wrong. The MTBF of a computer hard disc, for example, is around 150,000 hours.

multimedia computer system that combines audio and video components to create an interactive application that uses text, sound, and graphics (still, animated, and video sequences). For example, a multimedia database of musical instruments may allow a user not only to search and retrieve text about a particular instrument but also to see pictures of it and hear it play a piece of music.

As graphics, video, and audio are extremely demanding of storage space, multimedia PCs are frequently fitted with ◊CD-ROM drives because of the high storage capacity of CD-ROM discs. *See feature overleaf.*

A guide to multimedia

Multimedia discs look like music CDs – but instead of just playing music, they combine text, pictures, sound, and video. You can play multimedia discs on a personal computer as long as your computer meets certain specifications.

Why is multimedia such an exciting development?

Multimedia is a breakthrough in the world of computing. It allows information to be delivered in a totally new and highly effective way.

Imagine, for example, that you are interested in music and want to find out more about particular composers. In the comfort of your home you can switch on your PC and select an appropriate multimedia disc – such as *The Hutchinson Multimedia Encyclopedia*. In seconds you locate the entry on Beethoven, and the text of the article is displayed on your screen. If you want you can display a picture of Beethoven, and you can listen to an extract from his music. The article includes a cross-reference to Haydn: you can jump to the new article, read about Haydn's life, and hear an extract from Haydn's work.

You can continue like this for as long as you like, jumping between related concepts in a way which would be slow or impossible with a printed book. As you move between articles, the combination of text, pictures, video, and sound reinforces the message very strongly – far more strongly, for example, than text alone.

What were the beginnings of multimedia?

The first multimedia systems were based on videodisc technology. The videodisc has been largely superseded by a variety of compact disc technologies, of which CD-ROM (Compact Disc Read-Only Memory) is at present the most common.

CD-ROM evolved as a direct spin-off from the highly successful CD music disc, which is capable of delivering up to 72 minutes of high-quality music. Soon after music CDs were launched in 1982, it was discovered that a medium for storing high-quality audio could also be used, with some modifications, for storing large amounts of computer data. CD-ROM came onto the market in 1984. Unlike CD audio, CD-ROM discs can be played on personal computers with the addition of CD-ROM hardware and software.

At first, CD-ROM was used mainly for storing and delivering text. The format has been further developed so that it is now capable of delivering multimedia information.

Will CD-ROM continue to grow?

CD-ROM is now firmly established in the market-place. In 1986 there were fewer than 100 commercial CD-ROM titles: in 1994 the number had jumped from 100 to an estimated 9,500, including many multimedia titles. It seems likely that the number of new CD-ROM titles will continue to rise rapidly.

Can I play a multimedia CD-ROM on my PC?

Yes you can, provided that you have the appropriate CD-ROM hardware and software installed.

Many of the latest generation of PCs come with an integral CD-ROM drive. In this case, all you need to do is to follow the publisher's instructions to install your multimedia disc. If your PC does not have an integral CD-ROM drive, you need to upgrade your PC to an MPC (a multimedia PC as specified by Microsoft).

You need the following to play a multimedia CD-ROM:

Basic PC computer: 80386 SX; 4Mb of RAM; 4Mb of hard disk space; floppy drive; SVGA monitor; MS-DOS Version 5 or above; Microsoft Windows Version 3.1 or above with Multimedia extensions.

In addition you need:

- An MPC compatible CD-ROM drive, attached to the computer via an interface board;
- A 16-bit MPC compatible sound board and headphones or speakers.

What about my Mac?

You can also play multimedia CD-ROMs on your Mac, provided that you have a CD-ROM drive. A sound card is not necessary.

The latest generation of Macs comes with an integral CD-ROM drive.

I've heard that you don't need a PC for some multimedia discs – you can use a TV set and stereo instead.

Besides CD-ROM, there are other compact disc technologies with multimedia capabilities. To play these discs, you need a proprietary player which plugs into the TV set and stereo system.

At present, none of the other compact disc technologies have the same established user base as CD-ROMs, and it is hard to judge whether or not they will be successful.

The main alternatives to CD-ROM are:

- CD-I (Compact Disc Interactive – launched 1987) The CD-I player can play CD-I discs and ordinary music CDs. Most CD-I titles under development are aimed at the home market and include interactive screen-based games, educational works for children, and popular reference titles.

- CDTV (Commodore Dynamic Total Vision – launched 1991) CDTV is a direct rival to CD-I. The CDTV player can play CDTV discs and music CDs. Like CD-I, most titles are aimed at the home consumer market.

- PhotoCD (launched 1992) The idea behind the PhotoCD is to allow the user to put up to 100 photos onto a PhotoCD disc, which can then be viewed on a TV screen. CD-ROM is a read-only storage medium, whereas PhotoCD is based on a new write-once technology. In the near future the PhotoCD disc format will allow the user to add graphics and sound.

Photo CD discs can be played on Kodak's own PhotoCD player which plugs into the TV. In addition, they can be played on CD-I players and PCs with the latest CD-ROM drives.

What are the prospects for multimedia?

The potential for multimedia is vast. It is ideal for training, for marketing purposes, and as an exciting educational tool for all ages, both in the workplace and at home.

As the cost of both the hardware and the discs themselves continues to drop, multimedia looks set to play an increasing role in the way information is distributed and used in the 90s and beyond.

multiplexer in telecommunications, a device that allows a transmission medium to carry a number of separate signals at the same time – enabling, for example, several telephone conversations to be carried by one telephone line, and radio signals to be transmitted in stereo.

In *frequency-division multiplexing*, signals of different frequency, each carrying a different message, are transmitted.

Electrical frequency filters separate the message at the receiving station. In *time-division multiplexing*, the messages are broken into sections and the sections of several messages interleaved during transmission. Pulse-code modulation allows hundreds of messages to be sent simultaneously over a single link.

multitasking or *multiprogramming* a system in which one processor appears to run several different programs (or different parts of the same program) at the same time. All the programs are held in memory together and each is allowed to run for a certain period.

For example, one program may run while other programs are waiting for a ▷peripheral device to work or for input from an operator.

The ability to multitask depends on the ▷operating system rather than the type of computer. Unix is one of the commonest.

multiuser system or *multiaccess system* an operating system that enables several users to access the same computer at the same time. Each user has a terminal, which may be local (connected directly to the computer) or remote (connected to the computer via a modem and a telephone line). Multiaccess is usually achieved by *time-sharing*: the computer switches very rapidly between terminals and programs so that each user has sole use of the computer for only a fraction of a second but can work as if she or he had continuous access.

N

NAND gate type of ◊logic gate.

netiquette (derived from *Internet etiquette*) behaviour guidelines evolved by users of the ◊Internet. The rules of netiquette include: no messages typed in upper case (considered to be the equivalent of shouting); new users, or new members of a ◊newsgroup, should read the frequently asked questions (FAQ) file before asking a question; no advertising via ◊USENET newsgroups.

Users who contravene netiquette can expect to receive ◊electronic mail flames (angry messages) pointing out the error of their ways. The Internet community is fiercely protective of netiquette.

Net, the abbreviation for *the ◊Internet*.

Netware leading ◊local area network operating system, supplied by Novell.

network a method of connecting computers so that they can share data and ◊peripheral devices, such as printers. The main types are classified by the pattern of the connections – star or ring network, for example – or by the degree of geographical spread allowed; for example, *local area networks* (LANs) for communication within a room or building, and *wide area networks* (WANs) for more remote systems. Internet is the computer network that connects major English-speaking institutions throughout the world, with around 12 million users. Janet (joint academic network), a variant of Internet, is used in Britain. SuperJanet, launched 1992, is an extension of this that can carry 1,000 million bits of information per second. One of the most common networking systems is Ethernet, developed in the 1970s (released 1980) at Xerox's Palo Alto Research Center, California, by Rich Seifert, Bob Printis, and Dave Redell. *See illustration overleaf.*

network
wide area network

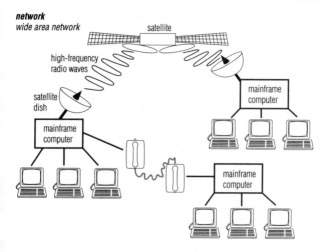

neural network artificial network of processors that attempts to mimic the structure of nerve cells (neurons) in the human brain. Neural networks may be electronic, optical, or simulated by computer software.

A basic network has three layers of processors: an input layer, an output layer, and a 'hidden' layer in between. Each processor is connected to every other in the network by a system of 'synapses'; every processor in the top layer connects to every one in the hidden layer, and each of these connects to every processor in the output layer. This means that each nerve cell in the middle and bottom layers receives input from several different sources; only when the amount of input exceeds a critical level does the cell fire an output signal.

The chief characteristic of neural networks is their ability to sum up large amounts of imprecise data and decide whether they match a pattern or not. Networks of this type may be used in developing robot vision, matching fingerprints, and analysing fluctuations in stock-

network
local area network

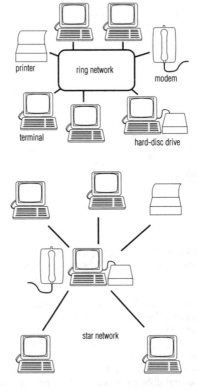

market prices. However, it is thought unlikely by scientists that such networks will ever accurately be able to imitate the human brain, which is very much more complicated; it contains around 10 billion nerve cells, whereas current artificial networks contain only a few hundred processors.

newgroup discussion group on the ◊Internet's ◊USENET. Newsgroups are organized in several broad categories, for example biz (business), news, rec (recreational subjects) and sci (science). Within these categories there is a hierarchy of subdivisions, so biz.comp contains computing newsgroups, of which biz.comp.software is the newsgroup concerned with software.

Newsgroups exist for almost any subject one might care to think of, whether serious or frivolous. Because USENET is completely uncensored, some of the newsgroups are inevitably tasteless and offensive to many users.

Newton small portable computer, also called a personal communicator, produced by ◊Apple. The Newton also incorporates handwriting recognition software. The Newton 120 was released 1995.

NeXTStep ◊operating system and development environment, originally created for the ◊NeXT Technology computer, but now available for other computers, including the IBM PC. NeXTStep is based on ◊Unix but contains a high level of ◊object-oriented programming. Many of the ideas incorporated in NeXTStep have found their way into mainstream operating systems.

NeXT Technology Inc US computer manufacturer founded by Steve ◊Jobs. NeXT's first product was an advanced computer (called NeXT) based on the ◊Motorola 68000 series of ◊microprocessors.

NeXT had limited commercial success, and has been discontinued, but its operating system and development environment, ◊NeXTStep, has been made available to other computers.

Nintendo Japanese ◊games console and software manufacturer. Nintendo's most successful game is Super Mario Brothers.

nonvolatile memory ◊memory that does not lose its contents when the power supply to the computer is disconnected.

NOR gate in electronics, a type of ◊logic gate.

notebook computer small ◊laptop computer. Notebook computers became available in the early 1990s and, even complete with screen and hard-disc drive, are no larger than a standard notebook.

notebook computer

trackball

NOT gate or *inverter gate* in electronics, a type of ◊logic gate.

Novell US ◊network operating system specialist. Novell's ◊NetWare operating system for IBM-compatible PCs dominates the market for ◊local area networks and is used as an industry standard.

In 1994, Novell acquired ◊WordPerfect Corp and bought Borland International's spreadsheet business in an effort to enter the application market as well as the operating system market, and thus to compete directly with ◊Microsoft.

null character character with the ◊ASCII value 0. A null character is used by some programming languages, most notably C, to mark the end of a character string.

null-modem special cable that is used to connect the ◊serial interface of two computers, so as to allow them to exchange data.

null string a string, usually denoted by '–', containing nothing or a ◊null character. A null string is used in some programming languages to denote the last of a series of values.

O

object linking and embedding (OLE) enhancement to ◊dynamic data exchange, which makes it possible not only to include live data from one application in another application, but also to edit the data in the original application without leaving the application in which the data has been included.

object-oriented programming (OOP) computer programming based on 'objects', in which data are closely linked to the procedures that operate on them. For example, a circle on the screen might be an object: it has data, such as a centre point and a radius, as well as procedures for moving it, erasing it, changing its size, and so on.

The technique originated with the Simula and Smalltalk languages in the 1960s and early 1970s, but it has now been incorporated into many general-purpose programming languages.

object program the ◊machine code translation of a program written in a ◊source language.

OCR abbreviation for ◊*optical character recognition*.

octal number system number system to the base eight, used in computing. The highest digit that can appear in the octal system is seven. Normal decimal, or base-ten, numbers may be considered to be written under column headings based on the number ten. For example, the decimal number 567 stands for:

100s	10s	1s
(10^2)	(10^1)	(10^0)
5	6	7

Octal, or base-eight, numbers can be thought of as written under column headings based on the number eight. For example, the octal number 567 stands for:

64s	8s	1s
(8^2)	(8^1)	(8^0)
5	6	7

The octal number 567 is therefore equivalent to the decimal number 375, since $(5 \times 64) + (6 \times 8) + (7 \times 1) = 375$.

The octal number system is sometimes used by computer programmers as an alternative to the ◊hexadecimal number system.

off line not connected, so that data cannot be transferred, for example, to a printer. The opposite of ◊on line.

OMR abbreviation for ◊*optical mark recognition*.

on line connected, so that data can be transferred, for example, to a printer. The opposite of ◊off line.

on-line system originally a system that allows the computer to work interactively with its users, responding to each instruction as it is given and prompting users for information when necessary. Since almost all the computers used now work this way, 'on-line system' is now used to refer to large database, electronic mail, and conferencing systems accessed via a dial-up modem. These often have tens or hundreds of users from different places – sometimes from different countries – 'on line' at the same time.

opensystems systems that conform to ◊Open Systems Interconnection or ◊POSIX standards. ◊Unix was the original basis of open systems and most non-proprietary open systems still use this ◊operating system.

The term is also used more loosely to describe any system that can communicate with other systems and to describe other standards, such as ◊MS-DOS and ◊Windows. Open systems were developed partly to make better communication possible, but also to reduce users' dependence on (and lock-in to) suppliers of proprietary systems.

Open Systems Interconnection (OSI) International Standards Organization standard, defining seven layers of communication protocols. Although OSI is an international standard, existing protocols, such as ◊TCP/IP and IBM's ◊System Network Architecture are more commonly used in commercial systems.

Open Systems Interconnection (OSI): the seven layers of protocol

1.	Physical	concerns the mechanical, electrical and procedural interfaces involved between the terminal and the network
2.	Frame/Link	concerns the transmission in terms of data rather than bits, providing for the grouping of bits into bytes or frames
3.	Network	concerned with the efficient routeing of information
4.	Transport	concerns reliable communication between transmitting and receiving systems. Also concerns error-correction protocols
5.	Session	manages the dialogue between the communicating systems, turn management, synchronization, and so on
6.	Presentation	concerned with data formatting and code conversion; sets up agreed rules at the beginning of the connection; includes the language ASN 1
7.	Application	concerns applications, such as file transfer, electronic mail and directory services

operating system (OS) a program that controls the basic operation of a computer. A typical OS controls the Çperipheral devices, organizes the filing system, provides a means of communicating with the operator, and runs other programs.

Some operating systems were written for specific computers, but some are accepted standards. These include CP/M (by Digital Research) and MS-DOS (by Microsoft) for microcomputers. Unix (developed at AT&T's Bell Laboratories) is the standard on workstations, minicomputers, and supercomputers; it is also used on desktop PCs and mainframes.

In Nov 1994 IBM, Apple, and Motorola announced a joint venture to produce a 'common reference platform' personal computer, capable of running virtually all existing operating systems.

operations manager job classification for Çcomputer personnel. An operations manager coordinates all the day-to-day activities of the staff who run the computer applications.

operator job classification for Çcomputer personnel. A computer operator runs programs.

optical character recognition (OCR) a technique for inputting text to a computer by means of a document reader. First, a Çscanner produces a digital image of the text; then character-recognition software makes use of stored knowledge about the shapes of individual characters to convert the digital image to a set of internal codes that can be stored and processed by computer.

OCR originally required specially designed characters but current devices can recognize most standard typefaces and even handwriting. OCR is used, for example, by gas and electricity companies to input data collected on meter-reading cards.

optical computer computer in which both light and electrical signals are used in the ◊central processing unit. The technology is still not fully developed, but such a computer promises to be faster and less vulnerable to outside electrical interference than one that relies solely on electricity.

optical disc a storage medium in which laser technology is used to record and read large volumes of digital data. Types include ◊CD-ROM, ◊WORM, and erasable optical disc.

optical fibre very fine, optically pure glass fibre through which light can be reflected to transmit images or data from one end to the other. Although expensive to produce and install, optical fibres can carry more data than traditional cables, and they are less susceptible to interference.

Optical fibres are increasingly being used to replace metal communications cables, the messages being encoded as digital pulses of light rather than as fluctuating electric current. Bundles of optical fibres are also used in endoscopes to inspect otherwise inaccessible parts of machines or of the living body.

optical mark recognition (OMR) a technique that enables marks made in predetermined positions on computer-input forms to be detected optically and input to a computer. An *optical mark reader* shines a light beam onto the input document and is able to detect the marks because less light is reflected back from them than from the paler, unmarked paper.

OR gate in electronics, a type of ◊logic gate.

OS/2 single-user computer ◊operating system produced jointly by Microsoft Corporation and IBM for use on large microcomputers. Its main features are ◊multitasking and the ability to access large amounts of internal ◊memory.

It was announced 1987. Microsoft abandoned it 1992 due to its lack of market acceptance.

OSI abbreviation for ◊*Open Systems Interconnection*.

outline font ◊font in which the character outlines are defined, making the font scalable to any size. Outline fonts can be output using the resolution of the output device, unlike ◊bit map fonts, which can only be output at one size and one resolution. The most common forms of outline fonts are ◊PostScript and ◊TrueType.

output device any device for displaying, in a form intelligible to the user, the results of processing carried out by a computer.

The most common output devices are the ◊VDU (visual display unit, or screen) and the printer. Other output devices include graph plotters, speech synthesizers, and COM (computer output on microfilm/microfiche).

overflow error an ◊error that occurs if a number is outside the computer's range and is too large to deal with.

P

packet switching a method of transmitting data between computers connected in a ◊network. A complete packet consists of the data being transmitted and information about which computer is to receive the data. The packet travels around the network until it reaches the correct destination.

page-description language in computing, a control language used to describe the contents and layout of a complete printed page. Page-description languages are frequently used to control the operation of ◊laser printers. The most popular page-description languages are Adobe Postscript and Hewlett-Packard Printer Control Language.

page printer computer ◊printer that prints a complete page of text and graphics at a time. Page printers use electrostatic techniques, very similar to those used by photocopiers, to form images of pages, and range in size from small ◊laser printers designed to work with microcomputers to very large machines designed for high-volume commercial printing.

paging method of increasing a computer's apparent memory capacity. See ◊virtual memory.

parallel device a device that communicates binary data by sending the bits that represent each character simultaneously along a set of separate data lines, unlike a ◊serial device.

parallel processing emerging computer technology that allows more than one computation at the same time. Although in the 1980s this technology enabled only a small number of computer processor units to work in parallel, in theory thousands or millions of processors could be used at the same time.

Parallel processing, which involves breaking down computations into small parts and performing thousands of them simultaneously, rather than in a linear sequence, offers the prospect of a vast improvement in working speed for certain repetitive applications.

parallel running a method of implementing a new computer system in which the new system and the old system are run together for a short while. The old system is therefore available to take over from its replacement should any faults arise. An alternative method is ◊pilot running.

parameter variable factor or characteristic. For example, length is one parameter of a rectangle; its height is another. In computing, it is frequently useful to describe a program or object with a set of variable parameters rather than fixed values.

For example, if a programmer writes a routine for drawing a rectangle using general parameters for the length, height, line thickness, and so on, any rectangle can be drawn by this routine by giving different values to the parameters.

Similarly, in a word-processing application that stores parameters for font, page layout, type of ◊justification, and so on, these can be changed by the user.

parity of a number, the state of being either even or odd. In computing, the term refers to the number of 1s in the binary codes used to represent data. A binary representation has *even parity* if it contains an even number of 1s and *odd parity* if it contains an odd number of 1s.

parity

character	binary code	parity	base-ten representation
A	1000001	even	65
B	1000010	even	66
C	1000011	odd	67
D	1000100	even	68

For example, the binary code 1000001, commonly used to represent the character 'A', has even parity because it contains two 1s, and the binary code 1000011, commonly used to represent the character 'C', has odd parity because it contains three 1s. A *parity bit* is sometimes added to each binary representation to adjust its parity and enable a

◊validation check to be carried out each time data are transferred from one part of the computer to another. The parity bit is added as either a 1 or a 0 so that, after it has been added, every binary representation has the same parity. So, for example, the codes 1000001 and 1000011 could have parity bits added and become *0*1000001 and *1*1000011, both with even parity. If any bit in these codes should be altered in the course of processing the parity would change and the error would be quickly detected.

parity check a form of ◊validation of data.

PASCAL (acronym for *program appliqué à la selection et la compilation automatique de la littérature*) a high-level computer-programming language. Designed by Niklaus Wirth (1934–) in the 1960s as an aid to teaching programming, it is still widely used as such in universities, but is also recognized as a good general-purpose programming language. It was named after 17th-century French mathematician Blaise Pascal.

password secret combination of characters used to ensure ◊data security.

PC abbreviation for ◊*personal computer*.

PCI (abbreviation for *peripheral component interconnect*) form of ◊local bus connection between external devices and the main ◊central processing unit. Developed (but not owned) by ◊Intel, it was 32-bit 1993, but is to be extended to 64-bit.

PCL ◊page-description language, developed by Hewlett Packard for use on Laserjet laser printers. Versions PCL 1 to PCL 4 used ◊raster graphics fonts; PCL 5 uses ◊outline font.

PCMCIA (abbreviation for *Personal Computer Memory Card International Association*) standard for 'credit card' memory and device cards used in ◊portable computers. As well as providing ◊flash memory, PCMCIA cards can provide either additional disc storage, or modem or fax functionality.

PCX bitmapped ◊graphic file format, originally developed by Z-Soft for use with PC-Paintbrush, but now used and generated by many applications and hardware such as scanners.

pen-based computer computer (usually portable), for which input is by means of a pen or stylus, rather than a keyboard. It incorporates handwriting recognition software, although prior to the release of the Apple ◊Newton and similar models, this had effectively meant using separate characters rather than 'joined-up' writing.

Pentium microchip produced by ◊Intel 1993. The Pentium was designed to take advantage of the ◊PCI ◊local bus architecture, which increases the bandwidth available between devices.

An error in the 5 million Pentium chips manufactured 1993–Dec 1994 is expected to cost Intel at least $30 million to replace the chips.

Details of the P6 chip that will replace the Pentium were released Feb 1995. P6 contains 5.5 million transistors compared with Pentium's 3.1 million.

peripheral device any item of equipment attached to and controlled by a computer. Peripherals are typically for input from and output to the user (for example, a keyboard or printer), storing data (for example, a disc drive), communications (such as a modem), or for performing physical tasks (such as a robot).

personal computer (PC) another name for ◊microcomputer. The term is also used, more specifically, to mean the IBM Personal Computer and computers compatible with it.

The first IBM PC was introduced in 1981; it had 64 kilobytes of random access memory (RAM) and one floppy-disc drive. It was followed in 1983 by the XT (with a hard-disc drive) and in 1984 by the AT (based on a more powerful ◊microprocessor). Many manufacturers have copied the basic design, which is now regarded as a standard for business microcomputers. Computers designed to function like an IBM PC are *IBM-compatible computers*.

personal digital assistant (PDA) handheld computer designed to store names, addresses, and diary information. They aim to provide a more flexible and powerful alternative to the filofax or diary, but have met limited success.

Some PDAs (such as Apple's ◊Newton) can recognize the user's handwriting and store it as digital text (with variable accuracy). Less ambitious PDAs, such as the Psion Series 3, have achieved modest success.

personal identification device (PID) device, such as a magnetic card, carrying machine readable identification, which provides authorization for access to a computer system. PIDs are often used in conjunction with a ◊PIN.

PhotoCD picture storage and viewing system developed by Kodak and Philips. The aim of Kodak's PhotoCD is to allow the user to put up to 100 photos onto compact disc: images are transferred from film to a PhotoCD disc and can then be viewed by means of Kodak's own PhotoCD player, which plugs into a television set, or by using suitable software on a multimedia PC.

PhotoCD is based on the new ◊write-once technology. The images can be written to the disc in multiple recording sessions. Later versions of the PhotoCD format will allow the user to add graphics and sound.

PICT object-oriented file format used on the ◊Macintosh computer. The format uses ◊Quickdraw and is supported by almost all graphics applications on the Macintosh.

pilot running a method of implementing a new computer system in which the work is gradually transferred from the old system to the new system over a period of time. This ensures that any faults in the new system are resolved before the old system is withdrawn. An alternative method is ◊parallel running.

PIN (acronym for *personal identification number*) in banking, a unique number used as a password to establish the identity of a customer using an automatic cash dispenser. The PIN is normally encoded into the magnetic strip of the customer's bank card and is known only to the customer and to the bank's computer. Before a cash dispenser will issue money or information, the customer must insert the card into a slot in the machine (so that the PIN can be read from the magnetic strip) and enter the PIN correctly at a keyboard. This effectively prevents stolen cards from being used to obtain money from cash dispensers.

pixel (derived from *picture element*) single dot on a computer screen. All screen images are made up of a collection of pixels, with each pixel being either off (dark) or on (illuminated, possibly in colour). The number of pixels available determines the screen's resolution. Typical resolutions of microcomputer screens vary from 320×200 pixels to

pixel

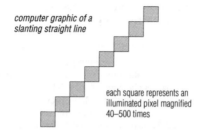

*computer graphic of a
slanting straight line*

each square represents an
illuminated pixel magnified
40–500 times

640 × 480 pixels, but screens with 1,024 × 768 pixels are now quite common for high-quality graphic (pictorial) displays.

The number of bits (binary digits) used to represent each pixel determines how many colours it can display: a two-bit pixel can have four colours; an eight-bit (one-byte) pixel can have 256 colours. The higher the resolution of a screen and the more colours it is capable of displaying, the more memory will be needed in order to store that screen's contents.

plasma display type of flat display, which uses an ionized gas between two panels containing grids of wires. When current flows through the wires a ◊pixel is charged causing it to light up.

platform the ◊operating system, together with the ◊hardware on which it runs.

plotter or *graph plotter* device that draws pictures or diagrams under computer control.

plotter

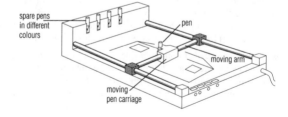

spare pens
in different
colours

pen

moving arm

moving
pen carriage

Plotters are often used for producing business charts, architectural plans, and engineering drawings. *Flatbed plotters* move a pen up and down across a flat drawing surface, whereas *roller plotters* roll the drawing paper past the pen as it moves from side to side.

point-of-sale terminal (POS terminal) computer terminal used in shops to input and output data at the point where a sale is transacted; for example, at a supermarket checkout. The POS terminal inputs information about the identity of each item sold, retrieves the price and other details from a central computer, and prints out a fully itemized receipt for the customer. It may also input sales data for the shop's computerized stock-control system.

polling a technique for transferring data from a terminal to the central computer of a ◊multiuser system. The computer automatically makes a connection with each terminal in turn, interrogates it to check whether it is holding data for transmission, and, if it is, collects the data.

pop-up menu a menu that appears in a (new) window when an option is selected with a mouse or key-stroke sequence in a ◊graphical user interface (GUI).

port a socket that enables a computer processor to communicate with an external device. It may be an *input port* (such as a joystick port), or an *output port* (such as a printer port), or both (an *i/o port*).

Microcomputers may provide ports for cartridges, televisions and/or monitors, printers, and modems, and sometimes for hard discs and musical instruments (MIDI, the musical instrument digital interface). Ports may be serial or parallel.

portability the characteristic of certain programs that enables them to run on different types of computer with minimum modification. Programs written in a ◊high-level language can usually be run on any computer that has a compiler or interpreter for that particular language.

portable computer computer that can be carried from place to place. The term embraces a number of very different computers – from those that would be carried only with some reluctance to those, such as ◊laptop computers and ◊notebook computers, that can be comfortably carried and used in transit.

POSIX (acronym for *portable operating system interface for computers – developed from Unix*) ◊American National Standards Institute standard, developed to describe how the programming interfaces and other features of ◊Unix worked, in order to remove control from the developers, AT&T Bell Laboratories. Subsequently many other (proprietary) ◊operating systems were modified in order to become POSIX-compliant, that is, they provide an ◊open systems interface, so that they can communicate with other POSIX-compliant systems, even though the operating systems themselves are internally quite different. See also ◊Open Systems Interconnection.

PostScript a page-description language developed by Adobe that has become a standard. PostScript is primarily a language for printing documents on laser printers, but it can be adapted to produce images on other types of devices.

PostScript is an object-oriented language, meaning that it treats images, including fonts, as collections of geometrical objects rather than as ◊bit maps. PostScript fonts are ◊outline fonts stored in the computer memory as a set of instructions for drawing the circles, straight lines and curves that make up the outline of each character. This means they are also scalable. Given a single typeface definition, a PostScript printer can thus produce a multitude of fonts.

The principal advantage of ◊vector graphics over bit-mapped graphics is that object-oriented images take advantage of high-resolution output devices whereas bit-mapped images do not. A PostScript drawing looks much better when printed on a 600 ◊dpi printer than on a 300 dpi printer. Object-oriented images also generally require less memory than bit-mapped images.

PowerPC ◊microprocessor produced by ◊Motorola as the successor to its 68000 series of microprocessors. It uses ◊RISC technology to provide great processing speed. The PowerPC chip was used in Apple's PowerMacintosh 1994.

printed circuit board (PCB) electrical circuit created by laying (printing) 'tracks' of a conductor such as copper on one or both sides of an insulating board. The PCB was invented in 1936 by Austrian scientist Paul Eisler, and was first used on a large scale in 1948.

Components such as integrated circuits (chips), resistors and capacitors can be soldered to the surface of the board (surface-mounted) or, more commonly, attached by inserting their connecting pins or wires into holes drilled in the board. PCBs include ◊motherboards, ◊expansion boards, and adaptors.

printer an output device for producing printed copies of text or graphics. Types include the ◊*daisywheel printer*, which produces good-quality text but no graphics; the ◊*dot matrix printer*, which produces text and graphics by printing a pattern of small dots; the ◊*ink-jet printer*, which creates text and graphics by spraying a fine jet of quick-drying ink onto the paper; and the ◊*laser printer*, which uses electrostatic technology very similar to that used by a photocopier to produce high-quality text and graphics.

Printers may be classified as *impact printers* (such as daisywheel and dot-matrix printers), which form characters by striking an inked ribbon against the paper, and *nonimpact printers* (such as ink-jet and laser printers), which use a variety of techniques to produce characters without physical impact on the paper.

A further classification is based on the basic unit of printing, and categorizes printers as character printers, line printers, or page printers, according to whether they print one character, one line, or a complete page at a time.

privacy the right of the individual to be free from secret surveillance (by scientific devices or other means) and from the disclosure to unauthorized persons of personal data, as accumulated in computer data banks. Always an issue complicated by considerations of state security, public welfare (in the case of criminal activity), and other factors, it has been rendered more complex by present-day technology.
computer data All Western countries now have computerized-data protection. In the USA the Privacy Act 1974 requires that there should be no secret data banks and that agencies handling data must ensure their reliability and prevent misuse (information gained for one purpose must not be used for another). The public must be able to find out what is recorded and how it is used, and be able to correct it. Under the Freedom of Information Act 1967, citizens and organizations have the right to examine unclassified files.

In Britain under the ◊Data Protection Act 1984 a register is kept of all businesses and organizations that store and process personal information, and they are subject to a code of practice set out in the act.

procedural programming programming in which programs are written as lists of instructions for the computer to obey in sequence. It closely matches the computer's own sequential operation.

procedure a small part of a computer program that performs a specific task, such as clearing the screen or sorting a file. A *procedural language*, such as BASIC, is one in which the programmer describes a task in terms of how it is to be done, as opposed to a *declarative language*, such as PROLOG, in which it is described in terms of the required result. See ◊programming.

Careful use of procedures is an element of ◊structured programming. In some programming languages there is an overlap between procedures, ◊functions, and ◊subroutines.

process control automatic computerized control of a manufacturing process, such as glassmaking. The computer receives ◊feedback information from sensors about the performance of the machines involved, and compares this with ideal performance data stored in its control program. It then outputs instructions to adjust automatically the machines' settings.

Because the computer can monitor and reset each machine hundreds of times each minute, performance can be maintained at levels that are very close to the ideal.

processing cycle the sequence of steps performed repeatedly by a computer in the execution of a program. The computer's CPU (central processing unit) continuously works through a loop, involving fetching a program instruction from memory, fetching any data it needs, operating on the data, and storing the result in the memory, before fetching another program instruction.

processor another name for the ◊central processing unit or ◊microprocessor of a computer.

program a set of instructions that controls the operation of a computer. There are two main kinds: ◊application programs, which carry out tasks for the benefit of the user – for example, word processing; and

◊systems programs, which control the internal workings of the computer. A ◊utility program is a systems program that carries out specific tasks for the user. Programs can be written in any of a number of ◊programming languages but are always translated into machine code before they can be executed by the computer. See ◊programming.

program documentation ◊documentation that provides a complete technical description of a program, built up as the software is written, and is intended to support any later maintenance or development of the program.

program flow chart type of ◊flow chart used to describe the flow of data through a particular computer program.

program loop part of a computer program that is repeated several times. The loop may be repeated a fixed number of times (*counter-controlled loop*) or until a certain condition is satisfied (*condition-controlled loop*). For example, a counter-controlled loop might be used to repeat an input routine until exactly ten numbers have been input; a condition-controlled loop might be used to repeat an input routine until the ◊data terminator 'XXX' is entered.

Program Manager the main screen, or 'front end', of the software product Microsoft Windows. All Windows operations can be accessed from Program Manager.

programmer job classification for ◊computer personnel. Programmers write the software needed for any new computer system or application.

programming writing instructions in a programming language for the control of a computer. *Applications programming* is for end-user programs, such as accounts programs or word-processing packages. *Systems programming* is for operating systems and the like, which are concerned more with the internal workings of the computer.

There are several programming styles:
procedural programming, in which programs are written as lists of instructions for the computer to obey in sequence, is by far the most popular. It is the 'natural' style, closely matching the computer's own sequential operation; *declarative programming*, as used in the

programming languages

language	main uses	description
Ada	defence applications	high level
assembler languages	jobs needing detailed control of the hardware, fast execution, and small program size	fast and efficient but require considerable effort and skill
BASIC (*b*eginners' *a*ll-purpose *s*ymbolic *i*nstruction *c*ode)	mainly in education, business, and the home, and among nonprofessional programmers, such as engineers	easy to learn; early versions lacked the features of other languages
C	systems programming; general programming	fast and efficient; widely used as a general-purpose language; especially popular among professional programmers
COBOL (*co*mmon *b*usiness- *o*riented *l*anguage)	business programming	strongly oriented towards commercial work; easy to learn but very verbose; widely used on mainframes
FORTH	control applications	reverse Polish notation language
FORTRAN (*for*mula *tran*slation)	scientific and computational work	based on mathematical formulae; popular among engineers, scientists, and mathematicians
LISP (*lis*t *p*rocessing)	artificial intelligence	symbolic language with a reputation for being hard to learn; popular in the academic and research communities
Modula-2	systems and real-time programming; general programming	highly structured; intended to replace Pascal for 'real-world' applications
OBERON	general programming	small, compact language incorporating many of the features of PASCAL and Modula-2
PASCAL (*p*rogram *a*ppliqué à la *s*élection et la *c*ompilation *a*utomatique de la *l*ittérature)	general-purpose language	highly structured; widely used for teaching programming in universities
PROLOG (*pro*gramming in *log*ic	artificial intelligence	symbolic-logic programming system, originally intended for theorem solving but now used more generally in artificial intelligence

programming language PROLOG, does not describe how to solve a problem, but rather describes the logical structure of the problem. Running such a program is more like proving an assertion than following a procedure; *functional programming* is a style based largely on the definition of functions. There are very few functional programming languages, HOPE and ML being the most widely used, though many more conventional languages (for example C) make extensive use of functions; *object-oriented programming*, the most recently developed style, involves viewing a program as a collection of objects that behave in certain ways when they are passed certain 'messages'. For example, an object might be defined to represent a table of figures, which will be displayed on screen when a 'display' message is received.

programming language in computing, a special notation in which instructions for controlling a computer are written. Programming languages are designed to be easy for people to write and read, but must be capable of being mechanically translated (by a ◊compiler or an ◊interpreter) into the ◊machine code that the computer can execute. Programming languages may be classified as ◊high-level languages or ◊low-level languages. See also ◊source language.

program trading in finance, buying and selling a group of shares using a computer program to generate orders automatically whenever there is an appreciable movement in prices.

PROLOG (acronym for *programming in logic*) high-level computer-programming language based on logic. Invented in 1971 at the University of Marseille, France, it did not achieve widespread use until more than ten years later. It is used mainly for ◊artificial intelligence programming.

PROM (acronym for *programmable read-only memory*) a memory device in the form of an integrated circuit (chip) that can be programmed after manufacture to hold information permanently. PROM chips are empty of information when manufactured, unlike ROM (read-only memory) chips, which have information built into them. Other memory devices are ◊EPROM (erasable programmable read-only memory) and ◊RAM (random-access memory).

prompt symbol displayed on a screen indicating that the computer is ready for input. The symbol used will vary from system to system and application to application. The current cursor position is normally next to the prompt. Generally prompts only appear in ◊command line interfaces.

protected mode operating mode of ◊Intel microprocessors (80286 and above), which allows multitasking and provides other features such as ◊extended memory and ◊virtual memory (above 1 Gbyte). Protected mode operation also improves ◊data security.

protocol an agreed set of standards for the transfer of data between different devices. They cover transmission speed, format of data, and the signals required to synchronize the transfer. See also ◊interface.

public-domain software any computer program that is not under copyright and can therefore be used freely without charge. Much of this software has been written in US universities, under government contract. Public-domain software should not be confused with ◊shareware, which is under copyright.

pull-down menu a list of options provided as part of a ◊graphical user interface. The presence of pull-down menus is normally indicated by a row of single words at the top of the screen. When the user points at a word with a ◊mouse, a full menu appears (is pulled down) and the user can then select the required option.

In some graphical user interfaces the menus appear from the bottom of the screen and in others they may appear at any point on the screen when a special menu button is pressed on the mouse.

Q

Quickdraw object-based graphics display system used by the Apple ◊Macintosh range of microcomputers. The use of Quickdraw gives most Macintosh applications the same ◊look-and-feel.

Quicktime multimedia utility developed by Apple, initially for the ◊Macintosh, but now also available for ◊Windows. Allows multimedia, such as sound and video, to be embedded in other documents.

QWERTY standard arrangement of keys on a UK or US typewriter or computer keyboard. Q, W, E, R, T, and Y are the first six keys on the top alphabetic line. The arrangement was made to slow typists down in the days of mechanical keyboards in order that the keys would not jam together. Other European countries use different arrangements, such as AZERTY and QWERTZ, which are more appropriate to the language of the country.

R

Raid (acronym for *redundant array of independent* (or *inexpensive*) *discs*) arrays of discs, each connected to a bus, that can be configured in different ways, depending on the application. Raid 1 is, for example, disc mirroring, while Raid 5 spreads every character between discs. Raid is intended to improve performance and data security.

RAM (acronym for *random-access memory*) a memory device in the form of a collection of integrated circuits (chips), frequently used in microcomputers. Unlike ◊ROM (read-only memory) chips, RAM chips can be both read from and written to by the computer, but their contents are lost when the power is switched off. Microcomputers of the 1990s may have 16–32 megabytes of RAM.

RAMdisc ◊RAM that has been configured to appear to the operating system as a disc. It is much faster to access than an actual hard disc and therefore can be used for applications that need frequent read and write operations. However, as the data is stored in RAM, it will be lost when the computer is turned off.

random access an alternative term for ◊*direct access*.

random number one of a series of numbers having no detectable pattern. Random numbers are used in ◊computer simulation and ◊computer games. It is impossible for an ordinary computer to generate true random numbers, but various techniques are available for obtaining pseudo-random numbers – close enough to true randomness for most purposes.

range check a ◊validation check applied to a numerical data item to ensure that its value falls in a sensible range.

raster graphics computer graphics that are stored in the computer memory by using a map to record data (such as colour and intensity) for every ◊pixel that makes up the image. When transformed (enlarged, rotated, stretched, and so on), raster graphics become ragged and suffer loss of picture resolution, unlike ◊vector graphics. Raster graphics are typically used for painting applications, which allow the user to create artwork on a computer screen much as if they were painting on paper or canvas.

raster image processor full name for printer program ◊RIP.

read-only storage a permanent means of storing data so that it can be read any number of times but cannot be modified. CD-ROM is a read-only storage medium; CD-ROMs come with the data already encoded on them.

real-time system a program that responds to events in the world as they happen. For example, an automatic-pilot program in an aircraft must respond instantly in order to correct deviations from its course. Process control, robotics, games, and many military applications are examples of real-time systems.

record a collection of related data items or *fields*. A record usually forms part of a ◊file.

recursion technique whereby a ◊function or ◊procedure calls itself into use in order to enable a complex problem to be broken down into simpler steps. For example, a function that finds the factorial of a number n (calculates the product of all the whole numbers between 1 and n) would obtain its result by multiplying n by the factorial of $n-1$.

redundancy duplication of information. Redundancy is often used as a check, when an additional check digit or bit is included. See also ◊validation.

register a memory location that can be accessed rapidly; it is often built into the computer's central processing unit.

Some registers are reserved for special tasks – for example, an *instruction register* is used to hold the machine-code command that the computer is currently executing, while a *sequence-control register* keeps track of the next command to be executed. Other registers are used for holding frequently used data and for storing intermediate results.

relational database ⟡database in which data are viewed as a collection of linked tables. It is the most popular of the three basic database models, the others being *network* and *hierarchical*.

relative (of a value), variable and calculated from a base value. For example, a *relative address* is a memory location that is found by adding a variable to a base (fixed) address, and a *relative cell reference* locates a cell in a spreadsheet by its position relative to a base cell – perhaps directly to the left of the base cell or three columns to the right of the base cell. The opposite of relative is ⟡absolute.

remote terminal a terminal that communicates with a computer via a modem (or acoustic coupler) and a telephone line.

remote terminal

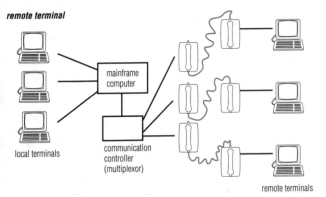

local terminals

mainframe
computer

communication
controller
(multiplexor)

remote terminals

reserved word word that has a special meaning to a programming language. For example, 'if' and 'for' are reserved words in most high-level languages.

resolution the number of dots per unit length in which an image can be reproduced on a screen or printer. A typical screen resolution for colour monitors is 75 dpi (dots per inch). A ⟡laser printer will typically have a printing resolution of 300 dpi, and ⟡dot matrix printers typically have resolutions from 60 dpi to 180 dpi. Photographs in books and magazines have a resolution of 1,200 dpi or 2,400 dpi.

response time the delay between entering a command and seeing its effect.

reverse video alternative term for ◊*inverse video*.

RGB (abbreviation of ***red–green–blue***) method of connecting a colour screen to a computer, involving three separate signals: red, green, and blue. All the colours displayed by the screen can be made up from these three component colours.

RIP (abbreviation for ***raster image processor***) program in a laser printer (or other high-resolution printer) that converts the stream of printing instructions from a computer into the pattern of dots that make up the printed page. A separate program is required for each type of printer and for each page description language (such as ◊PostScript or ◊PCL).

RIPs are very demanding programs because of the complexity of a typical printed page. It is not unusual for RIPs to run on extremely fast and powerful ◊RISC ◊microprocessors, which are sometimes more powerful than the processor in the computer attached to the printer.

RISC (acronym for ***reduced instruction-set computer***) a microprocessor (processor on a single chip) that carries out fewer instructions than other (◊CISC) microprocessors in common use in the 1990s. Because of the low number of ◊machine code instructions, the processor carries out those instructions very quickly.

RISC microprocessors became commercially available in the late 1980s, but are less widespread than traditional processors. The Archimedes range of computers, popular in schools, is based on RISC processors.

robot any computer-controlled machine that can be programmed to move or carry out work. Robots are often used in industry to transport materials or to perform repetitive tasks.

The first International Robot Olympics was held in Glasgow, Scotland in 1990. The world's fastest two-legged robot won a gold medal for completing a 3-m/ 9.8-ft course in less than a minute.

rogue value another name for ◊data terminator.

ROM (acronym for *read-only memory*) a memory device in the form of a collection of integrated circuits (chips), frequently used in microcomputers. ROM chips are loaded with data and programs during manufacture and, unlike ◊RAM (random-access memory) chips, can subsequently only be read, not written to, by computer. However, the contents of the chips are not lost when the power is switched off, as happens in RAM.

ROM is used to form a computer's permanent store of vital information, or of programs that must be readily available but protected from accidental or deliberate change by a user. For example, a microcomputer ◊operating system is often held in ROM memory.

root directory the top directory in a ◊tree-and-branch filing system. It contains all the other directories.

rounding error an ◊error that occurs when a decimal result is rounded up or down.

router device that enables dissimilar networks (such as ◊Ethernet and ◊Token Ring) to interconnect, provided there is a common protocol. Routers can be programmed to determine the fastest or most cost-effective route for data to travel. See also ◊bridge and ◊brouter.

RS-232 interface standard type of computer ◊interface used to connect computers to serial devices. It is used for modems, mice, screens, and serial printers.

run-time error alternative name for execution ◊error.

run-time system programs that must be stored in memory while an application is executed.

run-time version copy of a program that is provided with another application, so that the latter can be run, although it does not provide the full functionality of the program. An example is the provision of run-time versions of Microsoft ◊Windows with Windows applications for those users who do not have the full version of Windows.

S

SAA abbreviation for ◊*systems application architecture*.

sampling measurement of an ◊analogue signal at regular intervals. The result of the measurement can be converted into a ◊digital signal.

scalable font font that can be used at any size and any resolution, on a screen or hard-copy device, such as a laser printer or image setter. Scalable fonts are always ◊outline fonts.

scanner a device that can produce a digital image of a document for input and storage in a computer. It uses technology similar to that of a photocopier. Small scanners can be passed over the document surface by hand; larger versions have a flat bed, like that of a photocopier, on which the input document is placed and scanned.

Scanners are widely used to input graphics for use in ◊desktop publishing. If text is input with a scanner, the image captured is seen by the computer as a single digital picture rather than as separate characters. Consequently, the text cannot be processed by, for example, a word processor unless suitable optical character-recognition software is available to convert the image to its constituent characters. Scanners vary in their resolution, typical hand-held scanners ranging from 75 to 300 dpi. Types include flat-bed, drum, and overhead.

screen or *monitor* output device on which a computer displays information for the benefit of the operator. The commonest type is the cathode-ray tube (CRT), which is similar to a television screen. Portable computers often use ◊liquid crystal display (LCD) screens. These are harder to read than CRTs, but require less power, making them suitable for battery operation.

screen dump the process of making a printed copy of the current VDU screen display. The screen dump is sometimes stored as a data file instead of being printed immediately.

scrolling the action by which data displayed on a VDU screen are automatically moved upwards and out of sight as new lines of data are added at the bottom.

SCSI (acronym for *small computer system interface*) a ⟡parallel device used by the Apple Macintosh and an increasing number of MS-DOS-based personal computers for the connection of devices such as disc drives, printers, and CD-ROM drives. SCSI can support high data transfer rates. A new version, SCSI-2, can support even higher transfer rates.

searching extracting a specific item from a large body of data, such as a file or table. The method used depends on how the data are organized. For example, a binary search, which requires the data to be in sequence, involves first deciding which half of the data contains the required item, then which quarter, then which eighth, and so on until the item is found.

search request a structured request by a user for information from a ⟡database. This may be a simple request for all the entries that have a single field meeting a certain condition. For example, a user searching a file of car-registration details might request a list of all the records that have 'VOLKSWAGEN' in the ⟡field recording the make of car. In more complex examples, the user may construct a search request using operators like AND, OR, NOT, CONTAINING, and BETWEEN.

sector part of the magnetic structure created on a disc surface during ⟡disc formatting so that data can be stored on it. The disc is first divided into circular tracks and then each circular track is divided into a number of sectors.

security protection against loss or misuse of data; see ⟡data security.

seek time time taken for a read-write head to reach a particular item of data on a ⟡disc track.

Sega Japanese ⟡games console and software manufacturer. Sega's most successful game is Sonic the Hedgehog.

sensor a device designed to detect a physical state or measure a physical quantity, and produce an input signal for a computer.

For example, a sensor may detect the fact that a printer has run out of paper or may measure the temperature in a kiln.

The signal from a sensor is usually in the form of an analogue voltage, and must therefore be converted to a digital signal, by means of an ◊analogue-to-digital converter, before it can be input.

sequence-control register or *program counter* a special memory location used to hold the address of the next instruction to be fetched from the immediate access memory for execution by the computer (see ◊fetch–execute cycle). It is located in the control unit of the ◊central processing unit.

sequential file a file in which the records are arranged in order of a ◊key field and the computer can use a searching technique, like a ◊binary search, to access a specific record. See ◊file access.

serial device a device that communicates binary data by sending the bits that represent each character one by one along a single data line, unlike a ◊parallel device.

serial file a file in which the records are not stored in any particular order and therefore a specific record can be accessed only by reading through all the previous records. See ◊file access.

serial interface an ◊interface through which data is transmitted one bit at a time. Compare with ◊parallel device.

server computer used as a store of software and data for use by other computers on a ◊network. See ◊file server.

SGML abbreviation for ◊*Standard Generalized Markup Language*.

shareware software distributed for the cost of disc copying and distribution, principally so that users have the opportunity to test its functionality and ability to meet their requirements. If users plan to use the software, they are asked to pay a small registration fee (of the order of £25–50) directly to the author. This may bring additional functionality and documentation. Shareware is not copyright-free. Compare with ◊public-domain software.

silicon chip ◊integrated circuit with microscopically small electrical components on a piece of silicon crystal only a few millimetres square.

One may contain more than a million components. A chip is mounted in a rectangular plastic package and linked via gold wires to metal pins, so that it can be connected to a printed circuit board for use in electronic devices, such as computers, calculators, television sets, car dashboards, and domestic appliances.

In 1991 IBM launched the world's fastest high-capacity memory computer chip. SRAM (static random-access memory) can send or receive 8 billion ◊bits of information per second.

It 'reads' and 'writes' data to its circuits at the same time, instead of in separate processes as other chips do.

simulation short for ◊*computer simulation*.

Sinclair Clive 1940– . British electronics engineer who produced the first widely available pocket calculator, pocket and wristwatch televisions, a series of home computers, and the innovative but commercially disastrous C5 personal transport (a low cyclelike three-wheeled vehicle powered by a washing- machine motor).

site location at which computers are used. If a company uses only ◊IBM computers, for example, it is known as an IBM site.

Smalltalk the first high-level programming language used in ◊object-oriented programming applications.

smart card plastic card with an embedded microprocessor and memory. It can store, for example, personal data, identification, and bank-account details, to enable it to be used as a credit or debit card. The card can be loaded with credits, which are then spent electronically, and reloaded as needed. Possible other uses range from hotel door 'keys' to passports.

SNA abbreviation for ◊*System Network Architecture*.

snail mail ◊electronic mail term for the conventional postal service. E-mail can deliver messages within minutes while conventional postal services take at least a day.

soft-sectored disc another name for an unformatted blank disc; see ◊disc formatting.

software a collection of programs and procedures for making a computer perform a specific task, as opposed to ◊hardware, the physical components of a computer system. Software is created by programmers and is either distributed on a suitable medium, such as the ◊floppy disc, or built into the computer in the form of ◊firmware. Examples of software include ◊operating systems, ◊compilers, and applications programs, such as payrolls. No computer can function without some form of software.

software project lifecycle various stages of development in the writing of a major program (software), from the identification of a requirement to the installation, maintenance, and support of the finished program. The process includes ◊systems analysis and ◊systems design.

sorting arranging data in sequence. When sorting a collection, or file, of data made up of several different ◊fields, one must be chosen as the *key field* used to establish the correct sequence. For example, the data in a company's mailing list might include fields for each customer's first names, surname, address, and telephone number. For most purposes the company would wish the records to be sorted alphabetically by surname; therefore, the surname field would be chosen as the key field.

The choice of sorting method involves a compromise between running time, memory usage, and complexity. Those used include *selection sorting*, in which the smallest item is found and exchanged with the first item, the second smallest exchanged with the second item, and so on; *bubble sorting*, in which adjacent items are continually exchanged until the data are in sequence; and *insertion sorting*, in which each item is placed in the correct position and subsequent items moved down to make a place for it.

soundcard printed circuit board that, coupled with a set of speakers, enables a computer to reproduce music and sound effects. 16-bit soundcards give better reproduction than 8-bit soundcards, and usually offer stereo sound.

source language the language in which a program is written, as opposed to ◊machine code, which is the form in which the program's instructions are carried out by the computer. Source languages are classified as either ◊high-level languages or ◊low-level languages, according to whether each notation in the source language stands for many or only one instruction in machine code.

Programs in high-level languages are translated into machine code by either a ◊compiler or an ◊interpreter program. Low-level programs are translated into machine code by means of an ◊assembler program. The program, before translation, is called the *source program*; after translation into machine code it is called the *object program*.

source program a program written in a ◊source language.

spamming advertising on the ◊Internet by broadcasting to all ◊newsgroups regardless of relevance. Spamming is contrary to netiquette, the Net's conduct code, and is likely to result in the advertiser being bombarded by flames (angry messages), and 'dumping' (the downloading of large, useless files). Spamming is on the increase with 10 incidents Dec 1994 rising to 20 in Feb 1995.

speech recognition or *voice input* any technique by which a computer can understand ordinary speech. Spoken words are divided into 'frames', each lasting about one-thirtieth of a second, which are converted to a wave form. These are then compared with a series of stored frames to determine the most likely word. Research into speech recognition started in 1938, but the technology did not become sufficiently developed for commercial applications until the late 1980s.

There are three types: *separate word recognition* for distinguishing up to several hundred separately spoken words; *connected speech recognition* for speech in which there is a short pause between words; and *continuous speech recognition* for normal but carefully articulated speech.

speech synthesis or *voice output* computer-based technology for generating speech. A speech synthesizer is controlled by a computer, which supplies strings of codes representing basic speech sounds (phonemes); together these make up words. Speech-synthesis applications include children's toys, car and aircraft warning systems, and talking books for the blind.

speech writing system computing system that enables data to be input by voice. It includes a microphone, and ◊soundcard that plugs into the computer and converts the analogue signals of the voice to digital signals. Examples include DragonDictate, and IBM's Personal Dictation System released 1994.

The user must read sample sentences to the computer on first use to familiarize it with individual pronunciation. Early speech writers were very inaccurate and slow but by 1993 speeds of 60 words per minute with 95–99% accuracy were achievable.

spooling the process in which information to be printed is stored temporarily in a file, the printing being carried out later. It is used to prevent a relatively slow printer from holding up the system at critical times, and to enable several computers or programs to share one printer.

spreadsheet a program that mimics a sheet of ruled paper, divided into columns and rows. The user enters values in the sheet, then instructs the program to perform some operation on them, such as totalling a column or finding the average of a series of numbers.

Highly complex numerical analyses may be built up from these simple steps.

Spreadsheets are widely used in business for forecasting and financial control. The first spreadsheet program, Software Arts' VisiCalc, appeared 1979. The best known include Lotus 1–2–3 and Microsoft Excel.

sprite a graphics object made up of a pattern of ◊pixels (picture elements) defined by a computer programmer. Some ◊high-level languages and ◊applications programs contain routines that allow a user to define the shape, colours, and other characteristics of individual graphics objects. These objects can then be manipulated and combined to produce animated games or graphic screen displays.

SQL (abbreviation of *structured query language*) high-level computer language designed for use with ◊relational databases. Although it can be used by programmers in the same way as other languages, it is often used as a means for programs to communicate with each other.

Typically, one program (called the 'client') uses SQL to request data from a database 'server'.

Although originally developed by IBM, SQL is now widely used on many types of computer.

SRAM (acronym for *static random-access memory*) computer memory device in the form of a silicon chip used to provide ◊immediate access memory. SRAM is faster but more expensive than ◊DRAM (dynamic random-access memory).

DRAM loses its contents unless they are read and rewritten every 2 milliseconds or so. This process is called *refreshing* the memory. SRAM does not require such frequent refreshing.

stack a method of storing data in which the most recent item stored will be the first to be retrieved. The technique is commonly called 'last in, first out'.

Stacks are used to solve problems involving nested structures; for example, to analyse an arithmetical expression containing subexpressions in parentheses, or to work out a route between two points when there are many different paths.

stand-alone computer self-contained computer, usually a microcomputer, that is not connected to a network of computers and can be used in isolation from any other device.

Standard Generalized Markup Language International Standards Organization standard describing how the structure of a text can be identified so that it can be used, probably via ◊filters, in applications such as ◊desktop publishing and ◊electronic publishing.

start bit ◊bit used in ◊asynchronous communications to indicate the beginning of a piece of data.

stepper motor electric motor that can be precisely controlled by signals from a computer. The motor turns through a precise angle each time it receives a signal pulse from the computer. By varying the rate at which signal pulses are produced, the motor can be run at different speeds or turned through an exact angle and then stopped. Switching circuits can be constructed to allow the computer to reverse the direction of the motor.

By combining two or more motors, complex movement control becomes possible. For example, if stepper motors are used to power the wheels of a small vehicle, a computer can manoeuvre the vehicle in any direction.

Stepper motors are commonly used in small-scale applications where computer-controlled movement is required. In larger applications, where greater power is necessary, pneumatic or hydraulic systems are usually preferred.

stop bit ◊bit used in ◊asynchronous communications to indicate the end of a piece of data.

string a group of characters manipulated as a single object by the computer. In its simplest form a string may consist of a single letter or word – for example, the single word SMITH might be established as a string for processing by a computer. A string can also consist of a combination of words, spaces, and numbers – for example, 33 HIGH STREET ANYTOWN ALLSHIRE could be established as a single string.

Most high-level languages have a variety of string-handling ◊functions. For example, functions may be provided to read a character from any given position in a string or to count automatically the number of characters in a string.

structured programming in computing, the process of writing a program in small, independent parts. This makes it easier to control a program's development and to design and test its individual component parts. Structured programs are built up from units called *modules*, which normally correspond to single ◊procedures or ◊functions. Some programming languages, such as PASCAL and Modula-2, are better suited to structured programming than others.

subroutine a small section of a program that is executed ('called') from another part of the program. Subroutines provide a method of performing the same task at more than one point in the program, and also of separating the details of a program from its main logic. In some computer languages, subroutines are similar to ◊functions or ◊procedures.

supercomputer the fastest, most powerful type of computer, capable of performing its basic operations in picoseconds (thousand-billionths of a second), rather than nanoseconds (billionths of a second), like most other computers.

To achieve these extraordinary speeds, supercomputers use several processors working together and techniques such as cooling processors down to nearly absolute zero temperature, so that their components conduct electricity many times faster than normal. Supercomputers are used in weather forecasting, fluid and aerodynamics. Manufacturers include Cray, Fujitsu, and NEC.

Of the world's 500 most powerful supercomputers 232 are in the USA, 109 in Japan, and 140 in Europe, with 23 in the UK. Fujitsu announced the launch of the world's most powerful computer 1992; it can perform 300 billion calculations a second.

support environment a collection of programs (◊software) used to help people design and write other programs. At its simplest, this includes a ◊text editor (word-processing software) and a ◊compiler for translating programs into executable form; but it can also include interactive debuggers for helping to locate faults, data dictionaries for keeping track of the data used, and rapid prototyping tools for producing quick, experimental mock-ups of programs.

SVGA (abbreviation for *super video graphics array*) a graphic display standard providing higher resolution than ◊VGA. SVGA screens have resolutions of either 800×600 or $1,024 \times 768$.

swap to move segments of data in and out of memory. For fast operation as much data as possible is required in main memory, but it is generally not possible to include all data at the same time. Swapping is the operation of writing and reading from the backup store, often a special space on the disc.

SX suffix used to denote certain chips in ◊Intel's 80x86 range of ◊microprocessors. It was first used 1988 when Intel introduced the 80386SX, identical internally to the 80386 (renamed the 80386DX), but which communicated more slowly with the rest of the computer. However, this meant that it could also use the cheaper circuit boards associated with the 80286 processor, which meant that computers based on the 80386SX could be considerably cheaper than their ◊DX counterparts.

Subsequently, the 80486SX was introduced to complement the 80486DX. However, in this case the SX denoted the absence of a built-in mathematics ◊coprocessor rather than slower operation.

symbolic address a symbol used in ◊assembly language programming to represent the binary ◊address of a memory location.

symbolic processor computer purpose-built to run so-called symbol-manipulation programs rather than programs involving a great deal of numerical computation. They exist principally for the ◊artificial intelligence language ◊LISP, although some have also been built to run ◊PROLOG.

synchronous regular. Most communication within a computer system is synchronous, controlled by the computer's own internal clock, while communication between computers is usually ◊asynchronous. Synchronous telecommunications are, however, becoming more widely used.

syntax error ◊error caused by incorrect use of the programming language.

Syquest manufacturer of removal ◊hard disc drives. Syquest drives are most commonly associated with the Apple ◊Macintosh, and are used to transport large files from one location to another.

system flow chart type of ◊flow chart used to describe the flow of data through a particular computer system.

system implementation in computing, the process of installing a new computer system.

To ensure that a system's implementation takes place as efficiently and with as little disruption as possible, a number of tasks are necessary. These include ordering and installing new equipment, ordering new stationery and storage media, training personnel, converting data files into new formats, drawing up an overall implementation plan, and preparing for a period of either ◊parallel running or ◊pilot running.

System Network Architecture (SNA) a set of communication protocols developed by IBM and incorporated in hardware and software implementations. See also ◊TCP/IP and ◊Open Systems Interconnection (OSI).

systems analysis the investigation of a business activity or clerical procedure, with a view to deciding if and how it can be computerized. The analyst discusses the existing procedures with the people involved, observes the flow of data through the business, and draws up an outline specification of the required computer system. The next step is ◊systems design.

Systems in use in the 1990s include Yourdon, SSADM (Structured Systems Analysis and Design Methodology), and Soft Systems Methodology.

systems analyst alternative name for ◊analyst; see also ◊computer personnel.

systems application architecture (SAA) an IBM model for client–server computing. SAA makes use of ◊CUA (common user access) to ensure that commands and keystrokes are used consistently in different applications.

systems design the detailed design of an ◊applications package. The designer breaks the system down into component programs, and designs the required input forms, screen layouts, and printouts. Systems design forms a link between systems analysis and ◊programming.

systems program a program that performs a task related to the operation and performance of the computer system itself. For example, a systems program might control the operation of the display screen, or control and organize backing storage. In contrast, an ◊applications program is designed to carry out tasks for the benefit of the computer user.

System X in communications, a modular, computer-controlled, digital switching system used in telephone exchanges.

System X was originally developed by the UK companies GEC, Plessey, and STC at the request of the Post Office, beginning in 1969. A prototype exchange was finally commissioned in 1978, and the system launched in 1980. STC left the consortium in 1982.

T

Taligent joint ◊IBM/◊Apple project to develop an ◊object-oriented programming operating system. Taligent's rivals are ◊NeXTStep and ◊Cairo.

tape streamer a backing storage device consisting of a continuous loop of magnetic tape. Tape streamers are largely used to store dumps (rapid backup copies) of important data files (see ◊data security).

TCP/IP (abbreviation for *transport control protocol/Internet protocol*) set of network protocols, developed principally by the US Department of Defense. TCP/IP is widely used, particularly in ◊Unix and on the ◊Internet.

teleworking or *telecommuting* working from home rather than in an office, typically using a telephone, fax, and a personal computer connected to the office via a modem. The term was introduced in the 1980s. In 1991 an estimated 2 million people in Britain were teleworkers, threequarters of these part time.

terminal a device consisting of a keyboard and display screen (◊VDU) – or, in older systems, a teleprinter – to enable the operator to communicate with the computer. The terminal may be physically attached to the computer or linked to it by a telephone line (remote terminal). A 'dumb' terminal has no processor of its own, whereas an 'intelligent' terminal has its own processor and takes some of the processing load away from the main computer.

terminate and stay resident (TSR) term given to a program that remains in the memory – for example, a clock, calculator, or thesaurus. The program is run by the use of a ◊hot key.

test data data designed to test whether a new computer program is functioning correctly. The test data are carefully chosen to ensure that all possible branches of the program are tested. The expected results of running the data are written down and are then compared with the actual results obtained using the program.

T$_E$X (pronounced 'tek') text formatting and typesetting system, developed by Donald Knuth and widely used for producing mathematical and technical documents. Unlike ◊desktop publishing applications, T$_E$X is not ◊WYSIWYG, although in some implementations screen preview of pages is possible. It is ◊public-domain software.

text editor a program that allows the user to edit text on the screen and to store it in a file. Text editors are similar to ◊word processors, except that they lack the ability to format text into paragraphs and pages and to apply different typefaces and styles.

TIFF (acronym for *tagged image file format*) a ◊graphic file format.

tiling arrangement of ◊windows in a ◊graphical user interface system so that they do not overlap.

time-sharing a way of enabling several users to access the same computer at the same time. The computer rapidly switches between user ◊terminals and programs, allowing each user to work as if he or she had sole use of the system.

   Time-sharing was common in the 1960s and 1970s before the spread of cheaper computers.

toggle to switch between two settings. In software a toggle is usually triggered by the same code, so it is important that this code only has two meanings. An example is the use of the same character in a text file to indicate both opening and closing quotation marks; if the same character is also used to mean an apostrophe, then conversion, via a toggle switch, for a ◊desktop publishing system that uses different opening and closing quotation marks, will not be carried out correctly.

Token Ring protocol for ◊local area networks, developed by IBM.

topology the arrangement of devices in a ◊network.

touch screen an input device allowing the user to communicate with the computer by touching a display screen with a finger. In this way, the user can point to a required ◊menu option or item of data. Touch screens are used less widely than other pointing devices such as the ◊mouse or ◊joystick.

Typically, the screen is able to detect the touch either because the finger presses against a sensitive membrane or because it interrupts a grid of light beams crossing the screen surface.

touch sensor in a computer-controlled ◊robot, a device used to give the robot a sense of touch, allowing it to manipulate delicate objects or move automatically about a room. Touch sensors provide the feedback necessary for the robot to adjust the force of its movements and the pressure of its grip. The main types include the strain gauge and the microswitch.

trace a method of checking that a computer program is functioning correctly by causing the changing values of all the ◊variables involved to be displayed while the program is running. In this way it becomes possible to narrow down the search for a bug, or error, in the program to the exact instruction that causes the variables to take unexpected values.

Extra program instructions may have to be inserted to produce a trace, or a ◊utility program may be used to generate a trace automatically when the program is run.

track part of the magnetic structure created on a disc surface during ◊disc formatting so that data can be stored on it. The disc is first divided into circular tracks and then each circular track is divided into a number of sectors.

trackball ◊input device that carries out the same function as a ◊mouse, but remains stationary. In a trackball the ball controlling the cursor position is operated directly with the fingers.

transaction file a file that contains all the additions, deletions, and amendments required during ◊file updating to produce a new version of a ◊master file.

transducer device that converts one form of energy into another. For example, a thermistor is a transducer that converts heat into an electrical voltage, and an electric motor is a transducer that converts an electrical voltage into mechanical energy. Transducers are important components in many types of ◊sensor, converting the physical quantity to be measured into a proportional voltage signal.

transistor–transistor logic (TTL) the type of integrated circuit most commonly used in building electronic products. In TTL chips the bipolar transistors are directly connected (usually collector to base). In mass-produced items, large numbers of TTL chips are commonly replaced by a small number of ◊uncommitted logic arrays (ULAs), or logic gate arrays.

TTL circuits require a very stable DC voltage of between 4.75 and 5.25 volts.

translation program a program that translates another program written in a high-level language or assembly language into the machine-code instructions that a computer can obey. See ◊assembler, ◊compiler, and ◊interpreter.

transputer a member of a family of microprocessors designed for parallel processing, developed in the UK by Inmos. In the circuits of a standard computer the processing of data takes place in sequence; in a transputer's circuits processing takes place in parallel, greatly reducing computing time for those programs that have been specifically written for it.

The transputer implements a special programming language called OCCAM, which Inmos based on CSP (communicating sequential processes), developed by C A R Hoare of Oxford University Computing Laboratory.

tree-and-branch filing system a filing system where all files are stored within directories, like folders in a filing cabinet. These directories may in turn be stored within further directories. The root directory contains all the other directories and may be thought of as equivalent to the filing cabinet. Another way of picturing the system is as a tree with branches from which grow smaller branches, ending in leaves (individual files). *See illustration overleaf.*

Trojan horse a ◊virus program that appears to function normally but, while undetected by the normal user, causes damage to other files or circumvents security procedures.

The earliest appeared in the UK in about 1988.

tree-and-branch filing system

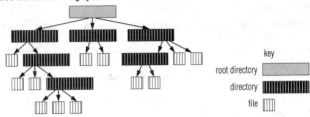

key

root directory

directory

file

TrueType a scalable font system, supplied as part of Microsoft ◊Windows 3.1. It allows scalable fonts to be used by non-PostScript printers. Such printers are usually cheaper.

truncation error an ◊error that occurs when a decimal result is cut off (truncated) after the maximum number of places allowed by the computer's level of accuracy.

truth table in electronics, a diagram showing the effect of a particular ◊logic gate on every combination of inputs.

Every possible combination of inputs and outputs for a particular gate or combination of gates is described, thereby defining their action in full. When logic value 1 is written in the table, it indicates a 'high' (or 'yes') input of perhaps 5 volts; logic value 0 indicates a 'low' (or 'no') input of 0 volts.

TSR abbreviation for ◊*terminate and stay resident*.

TTL abbreviation for ◊*transistor–transistor logic*, a family of integrated circuits.

turnaround document output document produced by a computer that is later, after additional data has been added, used as an input document.

For example, the meter-reading cards produced by gas and electricity companies form turnaround documents. Each card is output with customer details printed in a typeface readable by OCR (optical character recognition) and with a standard grid suitable for OMR (optical mark recognition). The meter reader inspects the customer's meter, marks the new reading on the grid, and then returns the card to the company's billing department. There, a ***universal document reader***, capable of reading both OCR and OMR data, is used to input the new information to the computer.

turnkey system system that the user has only to switch on to have direct access to application software that is usually specific to a particular application area. Turnkey systems often use menus. The user is expected to follow instructions on the screen and to have no knowledge of how the system operates.

turtle small computer-controlled wheeled robot. The turtle's movements are determined by programs written by a computer user, typically using the high-level programming language ◊LOGO.

turtle

floor turtle drawing a picture under computer control

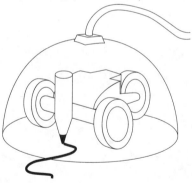

two's complement number system number system, based on the ◊binary number system, that allows both positive and negative numbers to be conveniently represented for manipulation by computer.

In the two's complement system the most significant column heading (the furthest to the left) is always taken to represent a negative number.

For example, the four-column two's complement number 1101 stands for:

$-8s$	$4s$	$2s$	$1s$
1	1	0	1

It is therefore equivalent to the decimal number -3, since $-8 + 4 + 1 = -3$.

U

ULA abbreviation for ◊*uncommitted logic array*, a type of integrated circuit.

unbundling marketing or selling products, usually hardware and software, separately rather than as a single package.

uncommitted logic array (ULA) or *gate array* a type of semi-customized integrated circuit in which the logic gates are laid down to a general-purpose design but are not connected to each other. The inter-connections can then be set in place according to the requirements of individual manufacturers. Producing ULAs may be cheaper than using a large number of TTL (◊transistor–transistor logic) chips or commissioning a fully customized chip.

undelete command that allows a user to reinstate deleted text or files. See also ◊delete.

underflow error an ◊error that occurs if a number is outside the computer's range and is too small to deal with.

Unicode proposed 16-bit character encoding system, intended to cover all characters in all languages (including Chinese and similar languages) and to be backwards compatible with ◊ASCII.

uninterruptible power supply (UPS) power supply that includes a battery, so that, in the event of a power failure, it is possible to continue operations. UPSs are normally used to provide time either for a system to be shut down in the usual way (so that files are not corrupted) or for an alternative power supply to be connected. For large systems these operations are usually carried out automatically.

Unix multiuser ◊operating system designed for minicomputers but becoming increasingly popular on large microcomputers, workstations, mainframes, and supercomputers. It was developed by AT&T's Bell Laboratories in the USA during the late 1960s, using the programming language ◊C. It could therefore run on any machine with a C compiler, so ensuring its wide portability. Its wide range of functions and flexibility have made it widely used by universities and in commercial software.

unshielded twisted pair (UTP) form of cabling used for ◊local area networks, now commonly used as an alternative to ◊coaxial cable.

UPS abbreviation for ◊*uninterruptible power supply*.

URL (abbreviation for *Uniform Resource Locator*) ◊World-Wide Web address. Web ◊browsers, such as ◊Mosaic, use URLs to locate documents on the Web. A typical URL, in this case for the Louvre's art gallery Web page, is http://mistral.enst.fr/~pioch/louvre/. The complexity of URLs explains why Mosaic's point-and-click interface, which saves the user from having to type them in, is so popular.

USENET (contraction of *users' network*) the world's largest ◊bulletin board system: a part of the ◊Internet. It consists of ◊electronic mail messages and articles organized into ◊newsgroups. It functions by bringing together people with common interests to exchange views and information. USENET is uncensored and governed by the rules of ◊netiquette.

user documentation ◊documentation that is provided to explain how to operate software.

user-friendly term used to describe the ease of use of a computer system, particularly for those with little understanding or familiarity with computers. Even for experienced users, user-friendly programs are quicker to learn.

user ID (contraction of *user id*entification) alternative name for ◊password.

user interface the procedures and methods through which the user operates a program. These might include ◊menus, input forms, error messages, and keyboard procedures. A ◊graphical user interface (GUI or WIMP) is one that makes use of icons (small pictures) and allows the user to make menu selections with a mouse.

utility program a systems program designed to perform a specific task related to the operation of the computer when requested to do so by the computer user. For example, a utility program might be used to complete a screen dump, format a disc, or convert the format of a data file so that it can be accessed by a different applications program.

UTP abbreviation for ◊*unshielded twisted pair*.

V

validation the process of checking input data to ensure that it is complete, accurate, and reasonable. Although it would be impossible to guarantee that only valid data are entered into a computer, a suitable combination of validation checks should ensure that most errors are detected.

Common validation checks include:

character-type check Each input data item is checked to ensure that it does not contain invalid characters.

For example, an input name might be checked to ensure that it contains only letters of the alphabet, or an input six-figure date might be checked to ensure it contains only numbers.

field-length check The number of characters in an input field is checked to ensure that the correct number of characters has been entered. For example, a six-figure date field might be checked to ensure that it does contain exactly six digits.

control-total check The arithmetic total of a specific field from a group of records is calculated – for example, the hours worked by a group of employees might be added together – and then input with the data to which it refers. The program recalculates the control total and compares it with the one entered to ensure that entry errors have not been made.

hash-total check An otherwise meaningless control total is calculated – for example, by adding together account numbers. Even though the total has no arithmetic meaning, it can still be used to check the validity of the input account numbers.

parity check Parity bits are added to binary number codes to ensure that each number in a set of data has the same ◊parity (that each binary number has an even number of 1s, for example). The binary numbers can then be checked to ensure that their parity remains the same. This check is often applied to data after it has been transferred from one part of the computer to another; for example, from a disc drive into the immediate-access memory.

check digit A digit is calculated from the digits of a code number and then added to that number as an extra digit. For example, in the ISBN (International Standard Book Number) 0 631 90057 8, the 8 is a check digit calculated from the book code number 063190057 and then added to it to make the full ISBN. When the full code number is input, the computer recalculates the check digit and compares it with the one entered. If the entered and calculated check digits do not match, the computer reports that an entry error of some kind has been made.

range check An input numerical data item is checked to ensure that its value falls in a sensible range. For example, an input two-digit day of the month might be checked to ensure that it is in the range 01 to 31.

variable a quantity that can take different values. Variables can be used to represent different items of data in the course of a program.

A computer programmer will choose a symbol to represent each variable used in a program. The computer will then automatically assign a memory location to store the current value of each variable, and use the chosen symbol to identify this location.

For example, the letter P might be chosen by a programmer to represent the price of an article. The computer would automatically reserve a memory location with the symbolic address P to store the price being currently processed.

Different programming languages place different restrictions on the choice of symbols used to represent variables. Some languages only allow a single letter followed, where required, by a single number. Other languages allow a much freer choice, allowing, for example, the use of the full word 'price' to represent the price of an article.

A *global variable* is one that can be accessed by any program instruction; a *local variable* is one that can only be accessed by the instructions within a particular subroutine.

VDU abbreviation for ◊*visual display unit*.

vector graphics computer graphics that are stored in the computer memory by using geometric formulas. Vector graphics can be transformed (enlarged, rotated, stretched, and so on) without loss of picture resolution. It is also possible to select and transform any of the components of a vector-graphics display because each is separately defined in the computer memory. In these respects vector graphics are superior to ◊raster graphics. Vector graphics are typically used for drawing applications, allowing the user to create and modify technical diagrams such as designs for houses or cars.

verification the process of checking that data being input to a computer have been accurately copied from a source document.

This may be done visually, by checking the original copy of the data against the copy shown on the VDU screen. A more thorough method is to enter the data twice, using two different keyboard operators, and then to check the two sets of input copies against each other. The checking is normally carried out by the computer itself, any differences between the two copies being reported for correction by one of the the keyboard operators.

Where large quantities of data have to be input, a separate machine called a *verifier* may be used to prepare fully verified tapes or discs for direct input to the main computer.

Veronica software tool for searching for files on the ◊Internet. Veronica is broadly similar to ◊Archie, but whereas the latter searches anonymous ◊ftp sites, Veronica searches ◊Gopher servers.

Veronica is sometimes said to stand for 'very easy rodent-oriented net-wide index to computerized archives'.

VGA (abbreviation for *video graphics array*) a colour display system that provides either 16 colours on screen and a resolution of 640 × 480, or 256 colours with a resolution of 320 × 200. ◊SVGA (Super VGA) provides even higher resolution and more colours.

video adapter an ◊expansion board that allows display of graphics and colour. Commonly used video adapters for IBM PC-based systems are Hercules, CGA, EGA, VGA, XGA, and SVGA.

videotext system in which information (text and simple pictures) is displayed on a television (video) screen. There are two basic systems, known as teletext and viewdata. In the teletext system information is broadcast with the ordinary television signals, whereas in the viewdata system information is relayed to the screen from a central data bank via the telephone network. Both systems require the use of a television receiver (or a connected VTR) with special decoder.

virtual without physical existence. Some computers have virtual memory, making their immediate access memory seem larger than it is; some computers can also simulate *virtual devices*. For example, the Acorn A3000 and A5000 computers have only one floppy-disc drive but can behave as if they were equipped with two, using part of the ◊RAM to simulate the second drive. ◊Virtual reality is a computer simulation of a whole physical environment.

virtual memory a technique whereby a portion of the computer backing storage, or external, ◊memory is used as an extension of its immediate access, or internal, memory. The contents of an area of the immediate access memory are stored on, say, a hard disc while they are not needed, and brought back into main memory when required.

The process, called paging or segmentation, is controlled by the computer ◊operating system and is hidden from the programmer, to whom the computer's internal memory appears larger than it really is. The technique can be successfully implemented only if very fast backing store is available, so that 'pages' of memory can be rapidly switched into and out of the immediate access memory.

virtual reality advanced form of computer simulation, in which a participant has the illusion of being part of an artificial environment. The participant views the environment through two tiny television screens (one for each eye) built into a visor. Sensors detect movements of the participant's head or body, causing the apparent viewing position to change. Gloves (datagloves) fitted with sensors may be worn, which allow the participant seemingly to pick up and move objects in the environment.

The technology is still under development but is expected to have widespread applications; for example, in military and surgical training, architecture, and home entertainment.

virus a piece of ◊software that can replicate and transfer itself from one computer to another, without the user being aware of it. Some viruses are relatively harmless, but others can damage or destroy data. They are written by anonymous programmers, often maliciously, and are spread along telephone lines or on ◊floppy discs. Antivirus software can be used to detect and destroy well-known viruses, but new viruses continually appear and these may bypass existing antivirus programs.

Computer viruses may be programmed to operate on a particular date, such as the Michelangelo Virus, which was triggered on 6 March 1992 (the anniversary of the birthday of Italian artist Michelangelo) and erased hard discs.

vision system computer-based device for interpreting visual signals from a video camera. Computer vision is important in robotics where sensory abilities would considerably increase the flexibility and usefulness of a robot.

Although some vision systems exist for recognizing simple shapes, the technology is still in its infancy.

Visual Basic computer language based on ◊BASIC.

visual display unit (VDU) computer terminal consisting of a keyboard for input data and a screen for displaying output. The oldest and the most popular type of VDU screen is the cathode-ray tube (CRT), which uses essentially the same technology as a television screen. Other types use plasma display technology and ◊liquid-crystal displays.

VLSI (abbreviation for *very large-scale integration*) in electronics, the early-1990s level of advanced technology in the microminiaturization of ◊integrated circuits, and an order of magnitude smaller than ◊LSI (large-scale integration).

voice input an alternative name for ◊speech recognition.

voice mail ◊electronic mail including spoken messages and audio. Messages can also be generated electronically using ◊speech synthesis.

voice output an alternative name for ◊speech synthesis.

volatile memory ◊memory that loses its contents when the power supply to the computer is disconnected.

VRAM (acronym for *video random-access memory*) form of ◊RAM that allows simultaneous access by two different devices, so that graphics can be handled at the same time as data is updated. VRAM improves graphic display performance.

W

WAIS (abbreviation for *Wide Area Information Server*) software tool for retrieving information from the ◊Internet. WAIS was the most powerful search tool on the Internet 1994 because of its ability to search for words within the text of documents; ◊Gopher and ◊Veronica, for example, only index files by keywords.

wait state situation when the ◊central processing unit or a ◊bus is idle. Wait states are necessary because system components run at different speeds.

WAN abbreviation for ◊*wide area network*.

wide area network (WAN) a ◊network that connects computers distributed over a wide geographical area.

Wilkes Maurice Vincent 1913– . English mathematician who led the team at Cambridge University that built the EDSAC (electronic delay storage automatic calculator) 1949, one of the earliest of the British electronic computers.

Wilkes was born in Dudley and studied at Cambridge. During World War II he became involved with the development of radar.

He was director of the Cambridge Mathematical Laboratory 1946–80.

In the late 1940s Wilkes and his team began to build the EDSAC. At the time, electronic computers were in their infancy. Wilkes chose the serial mode, in which the information in the computer is processed in sequence (and not several parts at once, as in the parallel type). This design incorporated mercury delay lines (developed at the Massachusetts Institute of Technology, USA) as the elements of the memory.

In May 1949 the EDSAC ran its first program and became the first delay-line computer in the world. From early 1950 it offered a regular computing facility to the members of Cambridge University, the first general-purpose computer service. Much time was spent by the research group on programming and on the compilation of a library of programs. The EDSAC was in operation until 1958.

EDSAC II came into service 1957. This was a parallel- processing machine and the delay line was abandoned in favour of magnetic storage methods.

WIMP (acronym for *windows, icons, menus, pointing device*) another name for ◊graphical user interface (GUI).

Winchester drive a small hard-disc drive commonly used with microcomputers; *Winchester disc* has become synonymous with ◊hard disc.

window a rectangular area on the screen of a ◊graphical user interface. A window is used to display data and can be manipulated in various ways by the computer user.

Windows ◊graphical user interface (GUI) from Microsoft that has become the standard for IBM PCs and clones using the ◊MS-DOS operating system.

Windows NT ◊multiuser and ◊multitasking operating system from Microsoft, based on ◊Windows. Unlike Windows, however, it does not need the intermediate layer of ◊MS-DOS. Windows NT is seen as a rival to ◊Unix.

word a group of bits (binary digits) that a computer's central processing unit treats as a single working unit. The size of a word varies from one computer to another and, in general, increasing the word length leads to a faster and more powerful computer.

Word word processing program for the IBM ◊PC and Apple ◊Macintosh produced by ◊Microsoft. Word began 1983 as an ◊MS-DOS program, but was much less successful than its rival, ◊WordPerfect and development ceased 1993. However, with the arrival of ◊Windows 3.0, Word for Windows established itself as the leading Windows word processor 1991.

WordPerfect word processing program for various computers produced by WordPerfect Corp. It was first released 1982 and by 1987 was the dominant ◊MS-DOS word processor, rapidly eclipsing the previous leader, WordStar, by offering many more features, despite having the reputation of being difficult to learn.

WordPerfect Corp was slow to release a version of WordPerfect for ◊Windows, and when it did appear 1992 it suffered in comparison with Microsoft ◊Word. Nevertheless, the rise of Windows led to development of the MS-DOS version being stopped 1994. In the same year, WordPerfect Corp was taken over by ◊Novell.

Versions of WordPerfect are also available for the ◊Macintosh, ◊OS/2 and ◊Unix, among others.

word processing storage and retrieval of written text by computer. Word-processing software packages enable the writer to key in text and amend it in a number of ways. A print-out can be obtained or the text could be sent to another person or organization on disc or via ◊electronic mail. Word processing has revolutionized the task of a typing secretary. Word-processing packages can be used with databases or graphics packages, and desktop publishing packages are available too.

word processor a program that allows the input, amendment, manipulation, storage, and retrieval of text; or a computer system that runs such software. Since word-processing programs became available to microcomputers, the method has been gradually replacing the typewriter for producing letters or other text.

Typical facilities include insert, delete, cut and paste, reformat, search and replace, copy, print, mail merge, and spelling check.

workstation high-performance desktop computer with strong graphics capabilities, traditionally used for engineering (◊CAD and ◊CAM), scientific research, and desktop publishing. Frequently based on fast RISC (reduced instruction-set computer) chips, workstations generally offer more processing power than microcomputers (although the distinction between workstations and the more powerful microcomputer models is becoming increasingly blurred). Most workstations use Unix as their operating system, and have good networking facilities.

World-Wide Web ◊hypertext system for publishing information over the ◊Internet. World-Wide Web documents are text files coded using ◊HTML so that they can include text, graphics, and sound, together with ◊hyperlinks to other Web documents. Web documents can be viewed using a browser, such as ◊Mosaic. The ease of use of the Web has led to a rapid expansion of the Internet; the Web was estimated 1994 to be growing at the rate of 1% per day.

WORM (acronym for *write once read many times*) a storage device, similar to ◊CD-ROM. The computer can write to the disc directly, but cannot later erase or overwrite the same area. WORMs are mainly used for archiving and backup copies.

write-once technology in computing, technology that allows a user to write data onto an optical disc once. After that the data is permanent and can be read any number of times.

write protection device on discs and tapes that provides ◊data security by allowing data to be read but not deleted, altered, or overwritten.

WYSIWYG (acronym for *what you see is what you get*) a program that attempts to display on the screen a faithful representation of the final printed output. For example, a WYSIWYG ◊word processor would show actual page layout – line widths, page breaks, and the sizes and styles of type.

X

X.500 directory standards for network addresses, issued by the ◊Comité Consultatif International Téléphonique et Télégraphique (CCITT).

XGA (abbreviation for *extended graphics array*) colour display system which is better than ◊VGA, providing either 256 colours on screen and a resolution of 1,024 × 768 or 25,536 colours with a resolution of 640 × 480.

XOR (contraction of e*x*clusive *OR*), a type of ◊logic gate. See also ◊Boolean algebra.

X-Windows ◊graphical user interface for Unix. X-Windows was developed at the Massachusetts Institute of Technology, and is ultimately intended to be a standard for windowing systems. X-Windows is now controlled by X-OPEN as part of the drive towards open systems in the Unix world.

Z

zero wait state term applied to ◊central processing units that run without wait states – that is, without waiting for slower chips.

ZIF socket (acronym for *zero insertion force socket*) socket on a computer's ◊motherboard that enables a chip to be easily removed or inserted by use of a lever. ZIF sockets are usually only used for expensive ◊microprocessors that are designed to be upgraded.

Appendices

computing: chronology

1614	John Napier invented logarithms.
1615	William Oughtred invented the slide rule.
1623	Wilhelm Schickard invented the mechanical calculating machine.
1645	Blaise Pascal produced a calculator.
1672–74	Gottfried Leibniz built his first calculator, the Stepped Reckoner.
1801	Joseph-Marie Jacquard developed an automatic loom controlled by punch cards.
1820	The first mass-produced calculator, the Arithometer, was developed by Charles Thomas de Colmar.
1822	Charles Babbage completed his first model for the difference engine.
1830s	Babbage created the first design for the analytical engine.
1890	Herman Hollerith developed the punched-card ruler for the US census.
1936	Alan Turing published the mathematical theory of computing.
1938	Konrad Zuse constructed the first binary calculator, using Boolean algebra.
1939	US mathematician and physicist J V Atanasoff became the first to use electronic means for mechanizing arithmetical operations.
1943	The Colossus electronic code-breaker was developed at Bletchley Park, England. The Harvard University Mark I or Automatic Sequence Controlled Calculator (partly financed by IBM) became the first program-controlled calculator.
1946	ENIAC (acronym for electronic numerator, integrator, analyser, and computer), the first general purpose, fully electronic digital computer, was completed at the University of Pennsylvania, USA.
1948	Manchester University (England) Mark I, the first stored-program computer, was completed. William Shockley of Bell Laboratories invented the transistor.
1951	Launch of Ferranti Mark I, the first commercially produced computer. Whirlwind, the first real-time computer, was built for the US air-defence system. Grace Murray Hopper of Remington Rand invented the compiler computer program.
1952	EDVAC (acronym for electronic discrete variable computer) was completed at the Institute for Advanced Study, Princeton, USA (by John Von Neumann and others).
1953	Magnetic core memory was developed.
1958	The first integrated circuit was constructed.
1963	The first minicomputer was built by Digital Equipment (DEC). The first electronic calculator was built by Bell Punch Company.
1964	Launch of IBM System/360, the first compatible family of computers. John Kemeny and Thomas Kurtz of Dartmouth College invented BASIC (Beginner's All-purpose Symbolic Instruction Code), a computer language similar to FORTRAN.
1965	The first supercomputer, the Control Data CD6600, was developed.

computing: chronology (continued)

1971   The first microprocessor, the Intel 4004, was announced.

1974   CLIP–4, the first computer with a parallel architecture, was developed by John Backus at IBM.

1975   Altair 8800, the first personal computer (PC), or microcomputer, was launched.

1981   The Xerox Star system, the first WIMP system (acronym for windows, icons, menus, and pointing devices), was developed. IBM launched the IBM PC.

1984   Apple launched the Macintosh computer.

1985   The Inmos T414 transputer, the first 'off-the-shelf' microprocessor for building parallel computers, was announced.

1988   The first optical microprocessor, which uses light instead of electricity, was developed.

1989   Wafer-scale silicon memory chips, able to store 200 million characters, were launched.

1990   Microsoft released Windows 3, a popular windowing environment for PCs.

1992   Philips launched the CD-I (Compact-Disc Interactive) player, based on CD audio technology, to provide interactive multimedia programs for the home user.

1993   Intel launched the Pentium chip containing 3.1 million transistors and capable of 100 MIPs (millions of instructions per second). The Personal Digital Assistant (PDA), which recognizes user's handwriting, went on sale.

1995   Intel releases details of the P6 microprocessor.

electronics: chronology

1897 The electron was discovered by English physicist John Joseph Thomson.

1904 English physicist Ambrose Fleming invented the diode valve, which allows flow of electricity in one direction only.

1906 The triode electron valve, the first device to control an electric current, was invented by US physicist Lee De Forest.

1947 John Bardeen, William Shockley, and Walter Brattain invented the junction germanium transistor at the Bell Laboratories, New Jersey, USA.

1952 British physicist G W A Dunner proposed the integrated circuit.

1953 Jay Forrester of the Massachusetts Institute of Technology, USA, built a magnetic memory smaller than existing vacuum-tube memories.

1954 The silicon transistor was developed by Gordon Teal of Texas Instruments, USA.

1958 The first integrated circuit, containing five components, was built by US electrical physicist Jack Kilby.

1959 The planar transistor, which is built up in layers, or planes, was designed by Robert Noyce of Fairchild Semiconductor Corporation, USA.

1961 Steven Hofstein designed the field-effect transistor used in integrated circuits.

1971 The first microprocessor, the Intel 4004, was designed by Ted Hoff in the USA; it contained 2,250 components and could add two four-bit numbers in 11-millionths of a second.

1974 The Intel 8080 microprocessor was launched; it contained 4,500 components and could add two eight-bit numbers in 2.5-millionths of a second.

1979 The Motorola 68000 microprocessor was introduced; it contained 70,000 components and could multiply two 16-bit numbers in 3.2-millionths of a second.

1981 The Hewlett-Packard Superchip was introduced; it contained 450,000 components and could multiply two 32-bit numbers in 1.8-millionths of a second.

1985 The Inmos T414 transputer, the first microprocessor designed for use in parallel computers, was launched.

1988 The first optical microprocessor, which uses light instead of electricity, was developed.

1989 Wafer-scale silicon memory chips were introduced: the size of a beer mat, they are able to store 200 million characters.

1990 Memory chips capable of holding 4 million bits of information began to be mass-produced in Japan. The chips can store the equivalent of 520,000 characters, or the contents of a 16-page newspaper. Each chip contains 9 million components packed on a piece of silicon less than 15 mm long by 5 mm wide.

1992 Transistors made from high-temperature superconducting ceramics rather than semiconductors produced in Japan by Sanyo Electric. The new transistors are 10 times faster than semiconductor transistors.

1993 US firm Intel launches the Pentium 64-bit microprocessor, with two separate integer processing units that can run in parallel, promising to be several times faster than earlier processors.

number systems

binary (base 2)	octal (base 8)	decimal (base 10)	hexadecimal (base 16)
0	0	0	0
1	1	1	1
10	2	2	2
11	3	3	3
100	4	4	4
101	5	5	5
110	6	6	6
111	7	7	7
1000	10	8	8
1001	11	9	9
1010	12	10	A
1011	13	11	B
1100	14	12	C
1101	15	13	D
1110	16	14	E
1111	17	15	F
10000	20	16	10
11111111	377	255	FF
11111010001	3721	2001	7D1

Thematic lists of computing terms

Computer architecture

Computer control

data processing

data representation

data storage

input devices

multimedia and interactivity

networks and the Internet

output devices

programming languages

systems analysis

software and applications

standards

computer architecture

accelerator board
access
access time
accumulator
adder
address
address bus
alpha
ALU
analogue computer
analytical engine
AND gate
Apple
arithmetic and logic unit
backup system
biological computer
BIOS
bistable circuit
bit pad
bridge
brouter
buffer
bus

cache memory
central processing unit
Centronics interface
CGA
chip
CISC
client–server architecture
clock interrupt
clock rate
CMOS
coaxial cable
command line interface
complementary metal-oxide
    semiconductor
computer
computer generation
configuration
console
control bus
control unit
coprocessor
copy protection
CPU
cylinder

data bus
decoder
dedicated computer
desktop
difference engine
digital computer
direct memory access
distributed processing
DRAM
edge connector
EEPROM
EGA
Ethernet
executable file
expanded memory
expansion board
extended memory
fetch–execute cycle
fifth-generation computer
file server
firmware
flag
flash memory
flip-flop
footprint
front-end processor
function key
gate
generation
gigabyte
GIS
hardware
HCI
hertz
high memory
hot key

HPGL
human–computer interaction
Hypercard
IBM
immediate access memory
information technology
instruction register
integrated circuit
Intel
interface
interrupt
ISA bus
LAN
laptop computer
LCD
LED
local bus
logic gate
LSI
Macintosh
mainframe
memory resident
microchip
microcomputer
microprocessor
Microsoft
MIDI
minicomputer
mips
monitor
motherboard
Motorola
multiuser system
multitasking
NAND gate
Netware

neural network
Newton
NOR gate
NOT gate
notebook computer
optical computer
OR gate
parallel processing
PC
PCI
PCMCIA
pen-based computer
Pentium
personal computer
platform
portable computer
Posix
printed circuit board
processing cycle
processor
PROM
protected mode
real-time system
register
RISC
RS-232 interface
run-time system
seek time
sequence-control register
serial interface
silicon chip
smart card
soft-sectored disc
SRAM
stand-alone computer
supercomputer

support environment
SVGA
synchronous
time-sharing
transistor–transistor logic
transputer
truth table
TTL
Turing machine
ULA
unbundling
uncommitted logic array
uninterruptible power supply
UPS
VGA
video adapter
VLSI
VRAM
WAN
Windows
Windows NT
XGA

computer control
ADC
analogue-to-digital converter
audit trail
autoexec.bat
backup
BIOS
Boolean algebra
carriage return
client–server architecture
command line interface
config.sys
console

copy protection
DAC
data logging
DDE
decimal number system
delete
desktop
digital-to-analogue converter
direct memory access
distributed processing
dongle
double click
dynamic data exchange
error detection
expanded memory
expansion board
extended memory
feedback (open-loop,
   closed-loop)
FAT
file server
formatting
groupware
HCI
hot key
HPGL
incremental backup
I/O
ISA bus
LAN
LCD
LED
local bus
memory resident
monitor (*n*)
monitor (*v*)

Motorola
MTBF
Netware
neural network
Newton
object linking and embedding
off line
on line
parallel interface
PCMCIA
pen-based computer
prompt
protected mode
Raid
router
sampling
SCSI
security
sensor
small computer system interface
soft-sectored disc
start bit
stepper motor
stop bit
support environment
SVGA
toggle
topology
touch sensor
turtle
undelete
uninterruptible power supply
UPS
UTP
VGA
video adapter

vision system
VRAM
wait state
WAN
Windows
Windows NT
zero wait state

data processing

batch processing
binary search
character type check
check digit
control total
data capture
data flow chart
data input
data preparation
data processing
data protection
data security
direct access
document
documentation
dump
EDP
EFTPOS
electronic mail
field
field-length check
file
file access
file generation
file merging
file searching
file sorting
file transfer
file updating
GIGO
grandfather–father–son system
hash total
indexed sequential file
justification
key field
key-to-disc system
logical error
master file
media
on-line system
parity check
password
PIN
random access
range check
record
searching
sequential access
serial file
sorting
transaction file
tree-and-branch filing system
turnaround document
user ID
validation
verification

data representation

acronym
alphanumeric data
analogue
ASCII
binary number code

binary number system
bit
bit map
bit-mapped font
block
byte
character
character set
control character
corruption of data
data
decimal number system
digit
digital
digital video interactive
dingbat
double precision
dumb terminal
EBCDIC
EIS
filter
floating-point notation
gate, logic
graphic file format
greeking
grey scales
hexadecimal number system
hinting
image compression
information technology
instruction set
interlacing
kilobyte
machine-readable
magnetic-ink character
    recognition

megabyte
null character
object linking and embedding
octal number system
outline font
parity
PCMCIA
PCX
PICT
PostScript
Quickdraw
Quicktime
QWERTY
redundancy
reverse video
scalable fonts
SGML
Standard Generalized Markup
    Language
T_EX
TIFF
tiling
transducer
TrueType
two's complement number system
typeface
Unicode
VRAM
word

data storage

access
access time
backing
bubble memory
cache memory

CD-R
CD-ROM
compact disc
data compression
data dictionary
defragmentation
digital audio tape
directory
disc
disc drive
disc formatting
Discman
disc optimizer
document image processing
EEPROM
EPROM
FAT
field
file
file allocation table
flash memory
floppy disc
floptical discs
formatting
fragmentation
gigabyte
graphic file format
hard disc
hard-sectored disc
image compression
immediate access memory
inverted file
JPEG
kilobyte
magnetic tape
mass storage system

media
megabyte
memory
nonvolatile memory
optical disc
paging
PCMCIA
Raid
RAM
RAMdisc
ROM
root directory
search request
sector
soft-sectored disc
tape streamer
track
volatile memory
Winchester drive
WORM
write protection

input devices
bar code
digitizer
document reader
graphical user interface
graphics tablet
GUI
input device
I/O
joystick
keyboard
light pen
machine-readable

magnetic-ink character recognition
magnetic strip
mark sensing
menu
MICR
mouse
OCR
OMR
optical character recognition
optical mark recognition
parallel interface
pen-based computer
QWERTY
serial interface
speech recognition
T_EX
trackball
transducer
user interface
voice input

multimedia and interactivity

AVI
CD-I
CD-ROM XA
CD-ROM
CD-ROM drive
CDTV
compact disc
data compression
DVI
edutainment
electronic publishing
fractal
HTML

hypertext
image compression
infotainment
interactive
interactive computing
interactive video
MPC
multimedia
PhotoCD
Quicktime
soundcard
video adapter
virtual reality

networking and the Internet

Archie
ARPAnet
bridge
brouter
browser
bulletin board
client–server architecture
CompuServe
computer terminal
cyberspace
DIANE
electronic mail
emoticon
Ethernet
FDDI
flame
ftp
gateway
Gopher
groupware
hacking

handshake
host
information superhighway
intelligent terminal
kermit
local area network
modem
monitor
Mosaic
multiplexer
Net, the
netiquette
Netware
network
newsgroup
null-modem
on-line system
Open Systems Interconnection
personal identification device
polling
remote terminal
router
server
snail mail
spamming
System Network Architecture
TCP/IP
telecommuting
terminal
Token Ring
topology
URL
USENET
Veronica
voice mail
WAIS

wide area network
World-Wide Web
X.500

output devices
bit map
bit-mapped font
bubble-jet printer
CD-R
CMYK
character printer
COM
computer output on
    microfilm/microfiche
daisywheel
Discman
dot matrix printer
DTP
dumb terminal
electronic publishing
encapsulated PostScript
EPS
font
graph plotter
graphic file format
greeking
grey scales
hard copy
hinting
impact printer
ink-jet printer
interlacing
inverse video
I/O
laser printer
LCD

LED
light-emitting diode
line printer
liquid-crystal display
microfiche
microform
monitor (*n*)
outline font
output device
page description language
page printer
parallel interface
PCL
PICT
pixel
plasma display
plotter
PostScript
printer
Quickdraw
Quicktime
raster graphics
resolution
reverse video
RGB
scalable fonts
screen dump
scrolling
serial interface
speech synthesis
spooling
TIFF
TrueType
typeface
vector graphics
voice output

programming
absolute
AI
algorithm
Applications Program Interface
argument
array
benchmark
beta version
Boolean algebra
bubble sort
bug
checksum
data terminator
debugging
decimal number system
decision table
declarative programming
driver
dry running
error
error message
execution error
filter
flow chart
function
functional programming
fuzzy logic
gate, logic
global variable
heuristics
hot key
HPGL
interrupt
iteration
jump

library program
local variable
loop
macro
memory resident
monitor (*v*)
neural network
null character
object linking and embedding
object-oriented programming
overflow error
parameter
pop-up menu
procedure
program
program documentation
program flow chart
program loop
programmer
programming
public-domain software
RAMdisc
random number
recursion
relative
reserved word
rogue value
rounding error
run-time error
shareware
sprite
stack
string
structured programming
subroutine
symbolic address

symbolic processor
syntax error
systems program
terminate and stay resident
test data
T_EX
toggle
trace
truncation error
TSR
Turing machine
underflow error
user documentation
variable
virtual
virtual memory
XOR

programming languages
ADA
ALGOL
assembler
assembly language
BASIC
C
C++
COBOL
command language
compiler
FORTRAN
fourth-generation language
high-level language
interpreter
LISP
LOGO
low-level language

machine code
mnemonic
object program
PASCAL
portability
procedural programming
programming language
PROLOG
Smalltalk
source language
source program
SQL
translation program

systems analysis
feasibility study
parallel running
pilot running
SAA
software project lifecycle
system flow chart
system implementation
systems analysis
systems analyst
systems application architecture
systems design
telecommuting
Turing machine
turnkey system
unbundling

software and applications
Acrobat
AI
API
application

applications package
applications program
Applications Program Interface
artificial intelligence
audit trail
backup
bit map
bit-mapped font
boot
bug
bulletin board
CAD
CAL
CAM
checksum
CMYK
CNC
computer-aided design
computer-aided manufacturing
computer-assisted learning
computer game
computer graphics
computer numerical control
computer simulation
CP/M
critical-path analysis
cursor
database
data dictionary
dBASE
DDE
delete
desktop publishing
dingbat
distributed processing dithering
document image processing

DOS
DTP
dynamic data exchange
EDI
EIS
electronic publishing
e-mail
emulator
encapsulated PostScript
EPS
expert system
export
fuzzy logic
gate, logic
geographical information
    systems
GIS
graphic file format
greeking
grey scales
groupware
hinting
hypertext
import
knowledge-based system
Lotus 1–2–3
mail merge
memory resident
Microsoft
monitor (*v*)
MS-DOS
multimedia
object linking and embedding
operating system
OS/2
outline font

PCI
PCX
PICT
pop-up menu
process control
program trading
public domain software
RAMdisc
relational database
robot
run-time system
run-time version
SAA
sampling
search request
SGML
simulation
software
software project lifecycle
spreadsheet
Standard Generalized Markup
    Language
systems application architecture
terminate and stay resident
T_EX
text editor
TIFF
tiling
toggle
tree-and-branch filing system
Trojan horse
TrueType
TSR
turnkey system
typeface
undelete

Unix
utility program
videotex
virtual reality
virus
Windows
Windows NT
word processor
WYSIWYG

standards
American National Standards
  Institute
ANSI
CCITT
Comité Consultatif International
  Téléphonique
IBM
ISO
Microsoft
Open Systems Interconnection
Posix
Windows NT